Pilgrimage
to PASCHA

A Daily Devotional for Great Lent

Archpriest Steven John Belonick

with Michele Constable and Michael Soroka

Second edition edited by Deborah Malacky Belonick

ANCIENT FAITH PUBLISHING   CHESTERTON, INDIANA

Second edition published by:
    Ancient Faith Publishing
    A Division of Ancient Faith Ministries
    P.O. Box 748
    Chesterton, IN 46304

Unless otherwise noted, Scripture quotations are taken from the New King
James Version, © 1979, 1980, 1982 by Thomas Nelson, Inc. Used by permis-
sion.

ISBN: 978-1-944967-96-3

Library of Congress Control Number: 2020952095

Printed in the United States of America

This volume is dedicated to seminarians of the Diocese of New England of the Orthodox Church in America who are pursuing the high calling of the Holy Priesthood with the intention of devoting themselves to the pastoral care of parishes,

and to the memory of Archpriest Steven John Belonick, who with all his heart dedicated himself to imitating the Good Shepherd, our Lord Jesus Christ (John 10:11–18).

Contents

Preface to the Second Edition

Some twenty-five years ago, Fr. Steven Belonick, my father confessor, priest, and friend, had the idea to compose a book of meditations and inspirational thoughts for Great Lent. I was honored and humbled to be asked to be part of that project, along with Michael Soroka, then choir director at our parish, Dormition of the Virgin Mary Church, in Binghamton, New York.

Father Steven told us, his coauthors, to compose heartfelt, sincere meditations. He instructed us to reach deeply into ourselves to realize our own sins and shortcomings and to admit them openly. He hoped in this way each of our readers might see themselves in a similar light and would journey with us on a common Christian pilgrimage.

Father Steven was an excellent spiritual guide. I remember our times working on this project as emotionally and psychologically intense. Certainly we shared fun and friendship, but more important was the spiritual growth we experienced. For me, the hardest part of composing the meditations was the struggle to admit my weaknesses and sins. Writing them on paper, then rereading and editing them, was much more demanding than even a sincere (and supposedly well-thought-out) recounting of my sins within the sacrament of Holy Confession!

Looking back over these meditations all these years later and anticipating their republication has shown me a lot about myself. I knew many of these meditations had profoundly touched me at the time I wrote them. I truly had reached deeply into my heart. Now as

I reread them, I also realize I still have the same shortcomings and sins as I did at the time of my writing them twenty-five years ago. But I also have the same goals for growth and a desire for forgiveness.

I still feel honored and grateful for the opportunity Fr. Steven gave me to participate in this venture. Republishing this book in his memory is a testimonial to his inspired priesthood—and to his excellent editing. He made our three voices ring out as one coherent expression, as two brothers and a sister on a common spiritual journey.

May new readers and old friends find God's grace as they accompany us once again on our Lenten pilgrimage. Especially, may those students in the Diocese of New England of the Orthodox Church in America—who will benefit from the special fund set aside to receive royalties from this book for their seminary education—be granted that grace. May they follow in the footsteps of a good pastor, Fr. Steven, and the one Good Shepherd, our Lord Jesus Christ.

May Archpriest Steven's memory be eternal!

—Michele Constable, coauthor

Preface to the First Edition

Church Tradition instructs us Christians to maintain a daily discipline of prayer. Likewise, it encourages us to read the Scriptures daily and to familiarize ourselves with the lives of the saints and the teachings of the Church Fathers, as well as writings of other recognized spiritual guides. These treasured tools of Tradition not only help us in the spiritual life, but also act as weapons against the devil, and, more importantly, they provide us with spiritual nourishment. They help to shape us as Christians, and there is no more appropriate period to pick up these tools and to allow this formation to begin than during the season of Great Lent.

Therefore, my two coauthors and I are offering you easily digestible daily nourishment from the Tradition of the Orthodox Church as you undertake your Lenten pilgrimage. Each portion in this little book contains a reference for a selected prescribed scriptural passage from either the Old or New Testament, a meditation on that scripture, practical advice from the Church Fathers and other saintly writers, an excerpt from a liturgical hymn, an edifying life of a saint, and a concluding prayer.

We are also offering you a variety of ways to fulfill your daily discipline. You may want to consume a full portion in one sitting, or you may want to read pieces of each portion throughout your day. You may easily digest some portions, while you may want to ponder over others. Do whatever benefits you. Be sure, however, to be faithful each day to your routine, and be sure to set aside some time, for the words in this book are not meant to be simply read and forgotten. They are meant to be reflected upon, digested, prayed about, and lived. Only by approaching them in this manner will your effort bear any spiritual fruit.

Finally, as we all begin this journey, let us remember one another in prayer, asking for each other God's mercy, guidance, and grace.

Yours in the Lord,
Archpriest Steven John Belonick

The funding for the publication of this volume has been provided by the Belonick and Taylor families in fond memory of Archpriest Steven John Belonick and his devotion to pastoral care.

DAY BEFORE GREAT LENT
Cheesefare/Forgiveness Sunday
SCRIPTURE READING: JOEL 2:12–26

Meditation

Today's scripture announces the threshold of the Great Fast. In the text—prescribed for the Wednesday before Great Lent—God calls His people to return to Him. In almost the same breath, He orders a period of fasting. Clearly, God's beckoning and His decree for a fast are connected.

God calls me back to Him, knowing my heart is far, far away. Similarly, I acknowledge my focus has strayed from Him—I have sought nourishment, happiness, security, and fulfillment everywhere and in everything but Him. And I realize: no matter how much "life" I try to consume, I am never really satisfied.

When I am honest with myself, I know I am far from Him, because my heart is stone cold. My prayer is weak, and I grow bored reading His Word. I go through the motions during church services, yet they have no effect on me. I am usually unhappy and complaining. I have no joy. Instead, I feel spiritually shipwrecked. Sometimes I feel nothing. My thoughts and emotions signal I have moved away from my Lord, who gives abundant life (see John 10:10).

Yet God is always calling me back, asking me to turn and to focus on Him. If I do, He will receive me gladly and provide the fulfillment that now escapes me.

To make this possible, God has set aside a fast—moments in time when I can turn from my usual activities and reflect and repent. He shows the way and provides the strength. Given His great grace and my meager effort, He will fill me with the life-giving spring of water my inner heart craves (John 4:14).

Font of Wisdom

As abbot of the Monastery of St. Mamas, St. Symeon the New Theologian (949–1022) instructed the monks under his charge daily, usually at the Matins service. His spiritual advice—captured in a body of works known as the *Discourses*—often included encouragement not only to seek God but also to accept His love. He describes the astounding effects of divine love:

> As soon as I called to mind the beauty of undefiled love, its light suddenly appeared in my heart. I have been ravished with its delight and have ceased to perceive outward things. . . . O all-desirable love, how happy is he who has embraced you, for he will no longer have a passionate desire to embrace any earthly beauty! Happy is he who is moved by divine love to cling to you! He will deny the whole world, yet as he associates with all men, he will be wholly untainted.

Upon meeting divine love, Symeon counts "the treasures of the world as nothing" and counts God alone as the font of "truly inexhaustible riches."

REFLECTION: *Let me count God as my prize possession and accept His love as I begin my interior Lenten pilgrimage.*

Hymn from Vespers

Let us not pray like the Pharisee: He who exalts himself will be humbled! Let us prepare to humble ourselves by fasting. Let us cry aloud with the voice of the publican: O God, forgive us sinners.

Mark the Ascetic of Egypt

Saint Mark the Ascetic came from a very wealthy family of merchants in fifth-century Athens. His family valued intellectual thought and scholarship, and they lovingly supported Mark when he chose to pursue religious knowledge rather than the family business.

Mark had the best education possible, due to his family's wealth and his outstanding academic ability. As he studied diligently and excelled in all areas of theological knowledge, he came to the attention of St. John Chrysostom, archbishop of Constantinople, who tutored him extensively. It was reported that Mark knew the whole Bible by heart!

Nine of his thirty discourses have come down to us. Three of them are included in Volume I of the English *Philokalia*. The Byzantines had such a high regard for his writings that they said, "Sell everything and buy 'Mark.'"

Mark's one desire was to attain spiritual perfection. He gave up the comfort of his family's wealth, loving support, and academic acclaim in order to seek union with God. He became an ascetic on a secluded mountaintop in Ethiopia, where he began to meditate, pray, fast, and write about religious concerns.

During sixty years of solitude and spiritual intensity, Mark became intimately attuned to the presence of the Holy Spirit and was completely filled with God's joy and holy peace. He reposed in the Lord at age 120.

PRAYER: *Lord, You have given me many blessings. Help me to follow the example of St. Mark by desiring in my heart to know You above all else.*

Meditation

When I'm stuck on how to resolve a problem, I stop ruminating and start from scratch. Usually, by getting a fresh look at a problem, I realize how to figure out a solution.

This same principle applies to my spiritual life. Each year during Great Lent the Church offers me time to return to a crucial starting point. I'm led back to the most important realities in life, since I do so poor a job of recalling them myself.

The scriptural reading for the first day of Great Lent takes me to the beginning of the Bible, the first verses of the Book of Genesis. Here I read that God created everything by His power and out of His great love. God is the source of all life. Everything comes from Him, finds its life in Him, and returns to Him.

So how is it I have come to live my life as if I am the center of everything, while I have shoved God away from His place of prominence and preeminence? Why do I prefer my own desires, thoughts, words, motives, and deeds above God's? When and how did I become my own god?

When I search my heart honestly, I realize what I really want is to control my own world. I want God, but only when His presence is convenient for me.

The period of Great Lent is meant to help me rediscover my priorities, beginning with my main priority—God Himself. It reminds me that God is God, and I am not. He is the source of all, and I am not. I am His creation, and He breathes life into me. To remember my proper relationship with Him comprises the first step in my Lenten spiritual pilgrimage.

Font of Wisdom

In his *Homily III On the Statues*, St. John Chrysostom (347–407), archbishop of Constantinople, urges his flock to prepare for spiritual warfare as Great Lent commences. He uses vivid imagery to motivate them: soldiers arming for battle, wrestlers stripping for a contest in the arena, and farmers preparing their sickles to prune back deadly weeds.

> *Put on the spiritual armor, and become a soldier. Strip yourself of worldly cares, for the season of Lent is one of wrestling. Cultivate your soul. Cut away the thorns of evil. Sow the word of godliness. Subdue the body, and bring it into subjection. Keep down the waves of evil desires. Repel the tempest of evil thoughts.*

His words mirror those of the Apostle Paul: "For we do not wrestle against flesh and blood, but against principalities, against powers, against the rulers of the darkness of this age, against spiritual *hosts* of wickedness in the heavenly *places*. Therefore take up the whole armor of God, that you may be able to withstand in the evil day, and having done all, to stand" (Eph. 6:12–13).

REFLECTION: *Let me zealously arm myself for spiritual warfare as I step onto the battlefield of Great Lent.*

Hymn from Vespers

Let us not only fulfill the fast in abstention from food. But let us be delivered from all material passions, having subdued the flesh that tortures us. That we may be worthy of communion with the Lamb—the Son of God who voluntarily was slain for the world—and spiritually celebrate the Savior's Resurrection from the dead. That we may be taken to the heights of virtue, making glad the Lover of All.

Gregory, Bishop of Nyssa

As the younger brother of Basil the Great and Macrina—both of whom also became saints—Gregory was raised by his siblings in Cappadocia after both their parents had died. Well-educated, Gregory taught rhetoric until he was urged to enter the priesthood by his friend, Gregory of Nazianzus, who also was eventually canonized.

In 372 Gregory was chosen to be the bishop of Nyssa in Cappadocia, located at the edge of his brother Basil's diocese in Caesarea. After Basil's death in 379, Gregory's stature rose; Emperor Theodosius valued Gregory's solutions to problems plaguing the Church.

Gregory's importance grew even more in 381 during the Second Ecumenical Council, the first of three such councils held in Constantinople. This particular council promulgated the Nicene Creed and worked diligently to quell the Arian heresy, which designated Jesus Christ as a creature rather than "Light of Light, and true God of true God," as the creed states.

The brothers Basil the Great and Gregory of Nyssa, along with their friend Gregory of Nazianzus, are revered as Fathers of the Church because of their defense of the Orthodox Faith during these troubling theological debates. Because of their common birthplace, the three are often referred to as the "Cappadocian Fathers."

Historians note Gregory died around 394. His legacy to the Church includes valuable writings describing the meaning of life and the Christian Faith, and also reflecting on nature's beauty—a love of creation he shared with his brother Basil.

PRAYER: *So often the doctrines of the Church seem far removed from the concerns of my daily life. Help me, Lord, to understand that I must know the teachings of my Faith in order to live it.*

Meditation

Mountains figure prominently in many Bible stories. I am reminded of Mount Sinai, where Moses received the Ten Commandments from God's hand; Mount Tabor, where Jesus led Peter, James, and John to witness His Transfiguration; and the hillside from which our Lord taught His famous Sermon on the Mount.

In all of these cases mountains express a theological principle— God reveals Himself and distributes divine gifts to those willing to rise above this world and seek a higher reality. Isaiah envisioned such an ascent when God spoke through him to call all people to "go up to the mountain of the Lord" (Is. 2:3), in today's reading.

Climbing a mountain takes a great deal of effort. It requires the right equipment. More importantly, it presumes that I am courageous and willing to attempt the climb. Great Lent can be likened to such a mountain. God calls me to ascend to Him. The journey is difficult and requires effort. Rather than boots and spikes, however, prayer, fasting, Scripture reading, quiet time, and a willing heart comprise my gear.

When mountaineers are asked why they brave the elements and dangers to scale a mountain, they sometimes simply respond, "Because it's there." Similarly, my explanation for undertaking a trying, uphill Lenten journey could be, "To ascend this mountain is not optional. This is where I will meet the Lord and receive true life from His hands." Surely, His gift is worth my effort to ascend.

Font of Wisdom

Saint Basil the Great (330–379), bishop of Caesarea, is known for his *Moralia* ("Morals") and his *Regula* ("Rules")—ethical manuals written for those living in the world and for those living as cloistered monks, respectively. Since Great Lent offers opportunity for an intensive inner pilgrimage, his words are beneficial for both lifestyles. In the *Rules*, St. Basil chides his readers for their lax efforts:

> *Although we suffer no hardship on behalf of the Lord's command, we, in the vanity of our minds, expect to achieve equal honor with those who have resisted sin even unto death. What man who sits at home or slumbers during the sowing ever filled the fold of his garment with sheaves at the harvest? Who has gathered grapes from a vine which he has not planted and tended? They who labor possess the fruits. Rewards and crowns belong to the victors.*

Through his exhortation, St. Basil recalls the Lord Jesus' words, "Blessed *is* that servant whom his master, when he comes, will find so doing" (Matt. 24:46).

REFLECTION: *Do I imagine my lackadaisical fasting, praying, and almsgiving will yield the same spiritual fruit as picking up my Cross and following in Christ's footsteps?*

Hymn from Matins

Let us begin the pure fast, which is the salvation of our souls. Let us serve the Lord with fear. Let us anoint our heads with the oil of good deeds. Let us wash our faces with the waters of purity. Let us not use empty phrases in prayer. But as we have been taught, let us cry out: Our Father in heaven, forgive us our trespasses, for You are the Lover of all.

Macarius the Great of Egypt

When the Roman Empire under Emperor Constantine legalized Christianity during the early fourth century, thousands of converts entered the Church and brought their worldly perspectives with them. Suddenly, it became easy to be a recognized as a Christian. For St. Macarius, however, this huge influx of new—and often luke-warm—"believers" became a regretful distraction. So he departed to the desolation of the desert to be alone with God.

Macarius had been born in Upper Egypt around 300. After tending cattle until he was thirty years old, he left for his desert skete, where he lived for the next sixty years. During his deliberate withdrawal from communal life, Macarius devoted his whole being to struggling against ungodly passions through an excessively austere, disciplined life. He solely desired to engage in prayer, which he viewed as the pinnacle of all ascetic practices. Thus he became one of the first teachers of "pure prayer"—the constant repetition of the name of the Lord, which later evolved into what is known as the Jesus Prayer: "Lord Jesus Christ, Son of God, be merciful to me, a sinner."

Macarius subsequently became the spiritual father of many holy monks who occupied separate hermitages in the desert. He recommended silence and continual prayer to his spiritual children. Always mild-mannered and patient, he taught that in prayer "there is no need to waste time with words; it is enough to hold out your hands and say, 'Lord, according to Your desire and to Your wisdom, have mercy.'"

PRAYER: *When I find it difficult to pray, Lord, make it easier by helping me to find simple but heartfelt words.*

WEDNESDAY   First Week of Great Lent

Scripture Reading: Genesis 1:24—2:3

Meditation

How often have you heard it said of someone, "How much he looks like his father!" or "Doesn't she resemble her mother?" In fact we often do resemble our parents and display many of their behaviors and mannerisms. Moreover, the older we get, the truer this seems!

God our Father made me in His image. This means I have the potential to resemble Him, and I have been called to do so throughout my lifetime. To resemble Him does not mean to look like Him physically, but instead to manifest His characteristics and His qualities as much as humanly possible.

Though I sometimes question whether or not this can be achieved, the Bible assures me it can. Hebrews 12:10 says I can share in His holiness. Second Peter 1:4 says I can be a partaker of His divine nature. Ephesians 4:13 speaks of my becoming Christlike. The First Epistle of John (3:2–3) assures me I can become like Him—purified from sin. I can exhibit God's love, compassion, forgiveness, light, wisdom, and mercy.

How is this possible? I must always remember these qualities are His, and He reveals His qualities through me, an earthen, pliable vessel. I must be willing to empty myself of the things that control me, especially the sin of pride. Then God will be able to fill me with Himself.

Great Lent gives me the tools to begin this work. God has endowed me with His image so that I am able grow into His likeness.

Font of Wisdom

In his Second Epistle, the Apostle Peter quotes a proverb: "'A dog returns to his own vomit,' and, 'a sow, having washed, to her wallowing in the mire'" (2 Pet. 2:22). Saint Gregory (335–after 384), bishop of Nyssa, brings this passage to mind in his treatise *On Virginity*. In this work he explains how the radiant image of God in a human being becomes besmeared through wrongdoing and evil intent.

> *It is like people who slip and fall in the mud and get their faces so smeared even their own relatives cannot recognize them. So man fell in the mud of sin, and he lost his likeness to God. In its stead he clothed himself in an image of clay—dry and mortal.*

Saint Gregory counsels his listeners to "wash away" this crusty image in the "purifying waters of the Christian life" so that "the soul's beauty will once again shine forth."

REFLECTION: *Having been made in God's image, let me leave my pigpen of destructive attitudes. Let me grasp His helping hand so I may once again exhibit His likeness.*

Hymn from Presanctified Liturgy

While fasting in body, let us also fast in spirit. Let us loose the bonds of iniquity. Let us undo chains of injustice. Let us break the yoke of oppression. Let us give food to the hungry. Let us shelter the poor and homeless, so that we may receive great mercy from Christ our God.

Theophylactus, Bishop of Nicomedia

Theophylactus, a late-eighth-century bishop of Nicomedia, was known as a peace-loving man of calm demeanor who worked constantly for the benefit of his people and their spiritual growth. During his episcopacy, the controversy over the use of icons in public and private worship raged, causing agonizing dissension within the Church. Emperor Leo the Armenian supported the iconoclasts, who opposed the veneration of icons.

Patriarch Nicephorus of Constantinople called on Bishop Theophylactus to lead a contingent of several bishops to approach Leo in order to persuade him that the iconoclasts' position was wrong. The bishops presented their theology respectfully, but Leo stubbornly shouted them down and declared that icons would be removed not only from churches and monasteries, but also from private homes.

Theophylactus spoke up determinedly against Leo, calling him a heretic who faced the wrath of God. In his anger, Leo exiled Theophylactus, who, refusing to recant, was banished to a desolate area for thirty years. He remained in disfavor with the empire's political powers until his death. However, Empress Theodora ordered the return of his body to Constantinople at the end of the iconoclastic period in 842, after the restoration of icons in both public and private worship.

PRAYER: *Lord, may I always acknowledge and defend You and Your Truth, without shame or fear.*

THURSDAY   First Week of Great Lent
SCRIPTURE READING: GENESIS 2:4–19

Meditation

From our days as toddlers and continuing throughout our adult lives, we have heard many warnings from relatives and friends. They may have cautioned us, "If you put your hands near the stove, you'll get burned," or "Don't drink and drive," or "Don't do any lifting with that bad back of yours."

Most of the warnings I have received in my life have been well founded and have been offered by people who love me. When I have failed to heed their advice, I have often experienced the bad consequences of my free choice.

In today's scripture I read of the creation of man and woman, the formation of human beings. And God gives Adam a clear warning: "Don't eat of the tree of the knowledge of good and evil, for if you do, you will die." Bear in mind: God did not offer Adam a threat, such as, "If you eat of that tree, I will kill you." God is not vindictive. He does not seek to hurt us human beings. But God does give Adam a warning, knowing that eating the fruit of that particular tree would bring separation from Him and, therefore, death. God warns Adam as a father would warn a beloved son.

This scripture reminds me that God warns me against doing, thinking, or acting in ways contrary to His will, out of His great love for me. He instructs, encourages, and invites me to live according to His will, knowing that only in doing so will I find true happiness. He knows that doing some things in my own misguided way will result in tragedy, and He hopes to spare me. My own experience, in fact, affirms this truth.

Font of Wisdom

A wonderful proverb to ponder is "Keep your heart with all diligence / For out of it *spring* the issues of life" (Prov. 4:23). Saint Seraphim of Sarov (1754–1833), a beloved Russian *staretz* (elder) renowned for his joyful spirit, brings to mind this passage in his spiritual counsel, preserved in *The Little Russian Philokalia, Volume I*. Writing about this proverb, he uses his vivid imagery:

> *The heart boils, being kindled by Divine fire, only when there is living water in it; but when this is poured out, it grows cold and a man freezes.*

Saint Seraphim warns his disciples to guard their hearts "from visible and invisible enemies," thus preserving what has been poured in by God. His words recall Jesus' teaching, "He who believes in Me, as the Scripture has said, out of his heart will flow rivers of living water" (John 7:38).

REFLECTION: *Am I hopeful God can turn my heart—stone-cold toward all who have wronged me—into a warm, loving vessel filled with forgiveness?*

Hymn from the Canon of St. Andrew of Crete

I have become an idol to myself, and in passions have I injured my soul. But accept me now in repentance, O Lord, and allow me to behold Your presence. May the enemy never possess me; may I never fall prey to him. O Savior, have mercy on me.

Holy Forty Martyrs of Sebaste

In 320, Licinius ruled the eastern part of the Roman Empire and Constantine ruled the western part. They had agreed, according to the Edict of Milan in 313, that Christianity would be permitted throughout the empire and that Christians would no longer be persecuted.

However, Licinius abruptly reneged on his agreement and reverted to paganism. He prepared his army to fight against Constantine, and fearing mutiny, he decided to remove all Christians from the ranks. He also decreed all Christians in the East would be tortured and slain if they did not give up their faith in Jesus Christ.

Forty soldiers of the twelfth legion of the Roman army stationed at Sebaste, Armenia, refused to disavow their faith by offering sacrifices to pagan gods. These soldiers were stripped naked and led onto a frozen pond, where bitter winds began to freeze them to death. Meanwhile, warm fires burned on the other side of the pond, enticing the cohort to weaken their resolve. Only one of the forty broke faith and fled toward the fires, and he died in his defection.

However, witnessing the faith and fortitude of the other soldiers, as well as a vision of angels crowning the dying martyrs, one of the pagan guards stripped down and walked out onto the pond to die as a Christian. His courage and newly lit faith kept intact the unit of forty men who died for Christ that day.

PRAYER: *Lord Jesus Christ, I claim to love You, but I cannot begin to imagine enduring torture or martyrdom. Help me to find even a tiny fraction of the zeal of the early martyrs, so that I will respond when You ask some small sacrifice from me.*

FRIDAY

First Week of Great Lent

SCRIPTURE READING: GENESIS 2:20—3:20

Meditation

Where *are* you?" (Gen. 3:9) God asks Adam and Eve after they have eaten the forbidden fruit and hidden from Him in the Garden. It is probably the most important question in the Bible!

God certainly knows where they are. His question, therefore, is one for Adam and Eve to contemplate. Their relationship with God changed when they disobeyed God's command and ate the fruit. Trust and faithfulness were broken. Now they are lost.

Being lost has nothing to do with geography. It is a condition of the heart resulting from a broken relationship with God. Being lost has to do with a sense of being cut off from God, a sense of alienation.

I feel lost when I choose to do things I know are contrary to His way. I feel lost when I willingly allow certain influences, rather than the Lord, to govern my life. I feel lost whenever I am satisfied to have a feeble, anemic relationship with God.

"Where *are* you?" Today I am offered this question, just as God posed it to Adam and Eve, with His same intention: love and concern for me. God actively and ceaselessly seeks me out, but He never attempts to force me to reconcile with Him. Instead, He asks me to contemplate: Where am I? Do I want to be found?

Great Lent provides me with the opportunity to reach out to the One who can save me. Instead of reaching out for deadly forbidden fruit, let me cling to His almighty and caring hand.

Font of Wisdom

Saint John Chrysostom, archbishop of Constantinople (347–407), draws on the words in today's Scripture reading in his *Homily XVII on the Book of Genesis*. His thunderous, dramatic sermon recounts the story of God seeking Adam and Eve in the Garden of Eden:

> *What has happened to Adam? I left you in one condition, whereas now I find you in another; I left you clad in glory, whereas now I find you in nakedness. . . .*
>
> *Who is responsible for depriving you of that wonderful garment you had the good fortune to wear? . . . What has happened to make you try to hide yourself from the One who has been so kind to you and who had placed you in a position of such importance?*

Saint John concludes that Adam and Eve themselves are responsible for their less-than-glorious state, for they have eaten from the "one tree" from which God had told them *not* to eat.

REFLECTION: *What's the "one thing" I've done that has set me on a path apart from God? Let me now recover my foothold on the narrower way God is placing before me.*

Hymn from Vespers

Come, O faithful. Let us perform the works of God in the light. Let us behave with decency as befits the day. Let us not make unjust accusations against our neighbors. Let us lay aside all fleshly pleasures and increase the spiritual gifts of our soul. Let us give food to those in need, drawing near to Christ and crying in repentance: O our God, have mercy on us!

Great-martyr Theodore the Recruit

Saint Theodore the Recruit (or "Tyro") is remembered twice in the Orthodox Church's calendar: on the date of his martyrdom in 306, and also on the first Saturday of Great Lent.

In Theodore's time Christians were harshly persecuted in the Roman Empire. Nevertheless, as a recently baptized young man and a new army recruit, he participated in frequent prayer and regular worship with other Christians. However, his role as a soldier and his belief as a Christian soon came into conflict.

While his legion wintered in quarters in the province of Pontus, Asia Minor, Theodore refused to join other soldiers in the customary pagan rites to honor the great success of his unit. Facing the governor of the province and the tribune of his legion, he boldly professed his faith in Jesus Christ not only by his words but also by his actions: the defiant Theodore set fire to a pagan temple in the city of Amasea. This act against Roman authority brought him merciless torture, and the brave recruit died in a burning furnace.

PRAYER: *Lord, St. Theodore found it impossible to keep his Christian faith separate from his daily occupations. Light a fire in my own heart so I too will acknowledge my faith in You, both in comfortable times and in times when I must speak up for Truth and suffer the consequences.*

SATURDAY   First Week of Great Lent

SCRIPTURE READING: MARK 2:23—3:5

Meditation

Jesus frequently angered the strict religious leaders of His day. Often He would seemingly break Sabbath laws, for example, either by healing the sick or by allowing His hungry disciples to pick grain to eat.

God's commandment to keep the Sabbath holy was one of the great Ten Commandments given to Moses (see Ex. 20:8). God instructed the people to work for six days but to cease from work on the seventh day. Since the word "work" was ambiguous, pious teachers of the Law attempted to define it. Through the centuries their definition of "work" became all encompassing to the point of absurdity; for instance, lifting anything on the Sabbath that weighed more than two dried figs was prohibited!

Jesus realized the legal experts of His day had distorted the meaning of God's Law. They had forgotten God's mercy and grace toward human beings when He made provision for the Sabbath. For the sake of ultra-piety, they had become insensitive to the purpose of God and to the sufferings of humanity.

I can identify with the legalists of Jesus' day. I am comfortable with rules, and I am very capable of using them—either for my own benefit or as a club against others. I find it easier to live and judge others by the letter of the Law rather than by its spirit, which intends that I should treat other people with mercy and grace.

Saint Isaac the Syrian observed that one must never call God "just." If He were just, then all human beings would be deemed unworthy and doomed. But God is *merciful*, and only by His compassion do I have hope in my salvation. Today, I beg God: Let me imitate Your mercy.

Font of Wisdom

In his *Ascetical Homilies*, St. Isaac the Syrian, a seventh-century bishop known for his strict fasting, writes about (of all things!) food. Recounting the story of Adam's expulsion from Paradise, St. Isaac identifies with the plight of his readers, who daily lived by the sweat of their brow in "a land of tares":

> *The tree of life is the love of God, from which Adam fell away, and thereafter he saw joy no longer, and he toiled and laboured in the land of tares. . . . Until we find love, our labour is in that land of tares, and in the midst of tares we both sow and reap, even if our seed is the seed of righteousness. . . . But once we find love, we partake of heavenly bread, and are made strong without labour and toil. The heavenly bread is Christ, Who came down from Heaven and gave life to the world.*

Saint Isaac tells his listeners that Jesus is the "bread of love," because "God is love" (1 John 4:16). By having God's love dwell in them, they can be refreshed at the banquet of His Kingdom, even while still on earth.

REFLECTION: *Let me allow God to turn my emotional hunger into spiritual hunger for Him as I try to avoid pathways that lead only to my numerous cravings.*

Hymn from Vespers

Come, all you who love the martyrs. Let us rejoice in spirit and celebrate. Today the martyr Theodore offers a mystical banquet, bringing joy to all who keep his memory. Rejoice, O Theodore, for you trampled underfoot the tyrant's threats.

Great-martyr Theodore the Recruit

Besides being revered for his martyrdom, Theodore the Recruit is honored for an event that took place in 362, some fifty-six years after his death. By that time Christianity had been a legal religion for a number of years, but Christians still faced many difficulties.

Julian the Apostate, the Roman emperor during that period and formerly a Christian himself, knew that Christians fasted very strictly during the first week of Great Lent in order to purify their senses. He surreptitiously commanded that the blood of sacrifices to idols be sprinkled on all the foodstuffs in the marketplace so that Christians would unwittingly consume the unclean food.

Through God's will, Theodore appeared in a dream to Eudoxius, archbishop of Constantinople, and made him aware of the defilement of the food in the marketplace. Theodore told Eudoxius to call the Christians together immediately to warn them of the unclean food and to tell them to eat easily prepared boiled wheat during that week instead. This allowed the Christians to maintain the fast and to be strengthened in their purpose. Sweetened boiled wheat is often brought to the church to be blessed and offered as food to the faithful on the first Saturday of Great Lent, in memory of this occasion.

PRAYER: *Strengthen me, Lord, with a simple desire to fast, and as I do so, please give me a foretaste of Your Kingdom.*

Sunday of the Triumph of Orthodoxy
SCRIPTURE READING: JOHN 1:43–51

Meditation

Christianity is less complicated than many make it out to be. The words of the Lord, the words of the gospel message, are very direct and understandable: "Follow Me" (Matt. 4:19); "Come and see" (John 1:46); "Take, eat" (Matt. 26:26); "Seek first the kingdom of God" (Matt. 6:33). Taking *action* regarding these words is the hard part.

Christ offered His message to everyday people. The disciples of Jesus were working people—fishermen, tax collectors, and so on. Yet the Church deems them wise, not because of their intellectual prowess, but because of their conscious decisions to apply His words to their lives. (Note the Troparion of the Feast of Pentecost, in which they are called "most wise.")

Jesus' disciples decided not just to hear His words, but also to act on them, to internalize them. And this changed everything. They realized following their Master did not mean simply watching what He did and gasping in amazement. They soon understood that to follow Jesus, the Christ, meant *to do* what He did and *to live* as He lived.

When will I cease being simply a spectator in my walk with Christ? When will I become one of Jesus' true disciples? A disciple takes what he learns from the master and lives it. I can begin living this reality by hearing a word He speaks, asking for His help in fulfilling it, acting on it daily to the best of my ability, and asking for His forgiveness when I fail, while never giving up. This is what God calls me to do and who He calls me to be.

Font of Wisdom

Saint Theophan the Recluse, bishop of Rostov (1815–94), played an important role in translating *The Philokalia*—a collection of writings from the Church Fathers—into the Russian language. A consistent thread weaving through *The Philokalia* is the art of interior prayer. Saint Theophan himself wrote several homilies on prayer. In his third sermon, he notes a familiar dilemma for anyone attempting to develop a prayer life:

> *We pray morning and evening. The time between is long. However ardently we pray, if we turn to God only at these times in a whole day and night, all will become scattered again. Then, when the time for prayer comes round, the soul will again be as cold and empty as before.*

"Even if we pray fervently," St. Theophan laments, "if we then keep cooling down and becoming distracted, what profit is there in it? We just create and destroy, create and destroy again: It is no more than empty labor."

The saint suggests three ways to avoid this useless cycle: dedicate some time in the morning to the contemplation of God; offer up every action in one's daily routine to the glory of God; and make frequent, heartfelt appeals to God, using short exclamations throughout the day, such as "Bless, O Lord" or "Save me, O Lord, I am perishing."

REFLECTION: *In my attempts at prayer, I seem to take one step forward but two steps backward. Let me confidently take "baby steps" in praying throughout my day, thus making my prayer life more vibrant.*

Hymn from Vespers

Today the Church receives honorable adornment—the holy icons of Christ, the Theotokos, and all the saints. The Church exults in their grace. We lift them up with joy and gladness.

Venerable Symeon the New Theologian

Symeon was born in 949 in Galatia. He was inspired from his youth by his spiritual father, Symeon the Studite, but he did not enter the monastery of Studios in Constantinople until he was twenty-seven years old, after having studied extensively.

Symeon became abbot of the nearby monastery of St. Mamas after his ordination to the priesthood, and he remained in this position for twenty-five years. As abbot, he implemented major reforms calling for a return to self-denial, asceticism, purity of heart, fasting, and constant prayer. His discourses to his monks on these topics never wavered in truth or zeal. Nevertheless, his strictness caused animosity and even harassment, which ultimately led to his exile.

Symeon was thoroughly grounded in the practice of the Jesus Prayer: "Lord, Jesus Christ, Son of God, be merciful to me, a sinner." However, he differed from other mystic saints in his forthright descriptions of his personal experiences with Christ. Symeon felt an intimacy and transformation in Christ and the presence of the Holy Spirit, and his writings vividly reflect his perceptions. Moreover, he expressed the conviction that *each Christian* must experience the presence and power of Christ. A personal mystical experience, he claimed, is available and should be the norm for all true Christians.

One of the prayers he composed regarding the reception of Holy Communion is among his most familiar works. It expresses his deep, enlivened relationship with God: "Those who fervently repent, You cleanse with the oil of love, causing them to shine, to share in Your light and in Your bounty. You grant that they become partakers of Your Divinity."

PRAYER: *Lord, I believe I have a relationship with You, but it is weak, and it needs to grow and to mature. Help me to desire intimacy with You.*

MONDAY   Second Week of Great Lent
SCRIPTURE READING: GENESIS 3:21—4:7

Meditation

Unlike their parents, Adam and Eve's sons Cain and Abel were not privileged to experience Paradise. According to the Old Testament Scripture, from birth the sons were destined to eke out their livings by hard work.

The Bible tells us that Cain, the elder of the two, tilled the ground. His brother Abel herded sheep. Both eventually understood that meeting up with God outside of Paradise was not as easy as it once had been inside. During those distant days, their parents had actually walked with God in the "cool of the day" (see Gen. 3:8). Now the two brothers came to understand that communion with God would require an offering from them to Him—a sacrifice.

The text tells us that God accepted Abel's offering but not Cain's. Why would God receive the gift of one but not the other? Because, this story teaches, it is not just *what* we offer to God that matters, but also *how* we offer it to Him. In other words, God knew full well the attitude and intention of Cain and Abel as they offered their gifts to Him, and He received them accordingly.

I can tell the difference between someone giving me something out of guilt—as appeasement, or simply because of duty—and someone giving me something out of love. Likewise, I know when *I* give something to someone whether it is out of duty or out of love! The former intention is cold and barren, and so is my gift. The latter intention is warm and caring, and my gift carries my heartfelt friendship to the receiver.

When I offer gifts to God or to the least of His brothers and sisters—prayer, service, talent, or money—I often have to admit my insincerity. I give out of habit or even out of guilt. The question I always need to ask myself is: How will God accept the intent of my offering?

Font of Wisdom

When St. Maximus the Confessor (580–662) wrote his *Four Hundred Chapters on Love*, he made astute observations about human nature based on Christ's Sermon on the Mount (see Matt. 5:1–11). He noted:

> *The world has many* poor in spirit, *but not as they should be; many that* mourn, *but over bad bargains or on account of the loss of children; many* meek, *but in the face of impure passions; many* hungering and thirsting, *but in order to seize others' goods and to gain unjustly. And there are many* merciful, *but toward the body and its comforts; many* clean of heart, *but for vanity's sake; many* peacemakers, *but they subject the soul to the flesh. The world has many that* suffer persecution, *but in an undisciplined manner; many that are* reviled, *but because of their shameful sins. [emphasis added]*

In his instruction on Jesus' Beatitudes, St. Maximus places great value on the intention of a person's heart. He urges his readers to have only God as their goal when they follow Christ's teachings; otherwise, he warns, "You will undergo toil and yet lose your reward."

REFLECTION: *As I examine my motives in practicing poverty of spirit, meekness of heart, willingness to be persecuted—and all the rest—am I being self-centered or God-centered?*

Hymn from Vespers

Enable us, O Lord, to continue well in the fast. Having permitted us to work in this time, O God, strengthen and restore our souls and bodies, so that having run the course in a virtuous manner, we may attain Your Resurrection!

Venerable Maximus the Confessor

Maximus is called "the Confessor" because of his labors and sufferings for the true Faith. He was one of the foremost pillars of Orthodoxy in the seventh century.

Born in 580, Maximus grew up in Constantinople. He became the principal secretary of Emperor Heraclius. He resigned his post because of the emperor's heretical opinions and then became a monk. After the death of Sophronius, patriarch of Jerusalem, who had been his spiritual father and teacher, Maximus took his place. In this role, he fought against the heresy of Monothelitism, a belief that Christ had only one will—a divine one. Maximus spent much of his life defending the Orthodox position that Christ had both a natural human will *and* a natural divine will, in that He possessed both a human and a divine nature.

Maximus found himself up against a most formidable defender of Monothelitism, Emperor Constans II, who decreed that this false doctrine be taught throughout his empire. As a supporter of the Orthodox position, Maximus was seized and charged with conspiring against the state.

Maximus endured many trials and sufferings in the years that followed. Most abominably, his tongue and right hand were mutilated so that he would cease preaching and writing. He was then exiled and died in 662, at the age of eighty-two, in Tsageri, which is in present-day Georgia. The Third Council of Constantinople upheld Maximus's theology, and he was venerated as a saint soon after his death.

PRAYER: *Lord, guide me as I confess my faith in You to others. Let my words be humble yet bold in proclaiming You as my Lord.*

TUESDAY   Second Week of Great Lent

SCRIPTURE READING: GENESIS 4:8–15

Meditation

Most North Americans view the US as a country built by rugged individualism. But all too often, promoting individualism can hinder a sense of community. Growing up with this embedded cultural heritage, US citizens are taught to keep their noses out of each other's business and to preserve individual rights at all costs.

At best, this societal norm might keep folks from becoming overbearing busybodies. At worst, it promotes isolation and noninvolvement, splinters communities, sparks intransigent political debates, and impedes opportunities for folks to resolve disagreements in a communal, respectful fashion.

Ironically, social media has further dulled our natural need to be social creatures. We fill hours with virtual conversations and often with virtual bullying, name calling, and argumentative diatribes.

This is not the way God meant human beings to live. He created us to be social beings, needing one another, helping one another, and supporting one another. God Himself is not an individual but a community of Persons, a Trinity one in nature and undivided in purpose.

Cain's cynical question to God in today's Scripture reading—*"Am I my brother's keeper?"* (Gen. 4:9)—is crucial to understanding how God wants me to live. If I am a Christian, then indeed, I believe we are keepers of one another. Saint Paul admonishes, "Let each of you look out not only for his own interests, but also for the interests of others" (Phil. 2:4).

I am created to complement others. Only in being the keeper of my brothers and sisters do I understand who I am as a person. Only through interaction do I discover my weaknesses, failings, and needs, as well as my talents and purpose.

Font of Wisdom

In his work *The Ascetic Life*, St. Maximus the Confessor (580–662) calls upon Christians to band steadfastly together in order to fight a common foe, Satan. He urges enlisting God as a helper while "banishing from ourselves the evil and unclean spirits." He writes:

> *Let us, who are harassed one by the other, grant pardon one to another, since we are all warred upon by the common enemy. Let us withstand our bad thoughts, calling upon God as our ally.*

The saint summons Christians to heartfelt love, sincerely leaving behind double-minded intentions and granting pardon to all. He exhorts his disciples to treat as brothers and sisters "those who hate and abominate us, that the Lord's name be glorified and manifest in its joyfulness"—for, he says, quoting St. Paul, "we are members of one another" (Eph. 4:25).

REFLECTION: *On Pascha night, when I hear these words from a Paschal hymn, "Let us call 'brethren' even those that hate us," will I be prepared to implement them with sincerity?*

Hymn from Vespers

The time of Lent is a time of gladness. With radiant purity and pure charity, filled with repentant prayer and all good deeds, let us sing with joy: "O most Holy Cross of Christ. . . enable us to bow down before you with pure hearts."

Basil the Great, Archbishop of Caesarea in Cappadocia

Basil was born in Caesarea, the capital of Cappadocia in Asia Minor, in 329, into an exceptional family. His grandmother, parents, three brothers, and a sister have been canonized as saints of the Orthodox Church. Another saint, Gregory of Nazianzus, a fellow student, was one of his best friends. Through the influence of his sister Macrina, Basil organized the first monastery in Asia Minor, and he established principles for the lives of Orthodox monastics: the *Greater Rules* and the *Lesser Rules*.

Basil lived during the rise of the Arian heresy, which claimed Jesus of Nazareth was not the divine Son of God but rather a created being. Basil was ordained a priest at Caesarea at the height of the heresy's popularity. He served Bishop Eusebius as an aide and a short time later became a bishop himself. He won over many foes by his patience and charity. Nevertheless, he spoke out strongly against the heresy, and he would not allow Arians to receive Holy Communion.

Basil was no less zealous in his pastoral duties. An eloquent orator, he preached mornings and evenings to vast congregations. His flock was in the habit of receiving Holy Communion four days of the week, and he encouraged them to assemble in church before sunrise to sing the Psalms. He organized a state-of-the-art hospital to serve the poor, which was famed for many years; some historians note it as the first hospital in history.

Basil died at age forty-nine, worn out by austerities, hard work, and ill health. His friend Gregory of Nazianzus mentioned Basil's establishment of the communal hospital at his funeral oration: "Basil's care was for the sick, and the relief of their wounds, and the imitation of Christ, by cleansing leprosy, not by a word, but in deed."

PRAYER: *Strengthen me, Lord, to be zealous in faith and good works in the face of difficulties.*

WEDNESDAY   Second Week of Great Lent

SCRIPTURE READING: ISAIAH 5:16–25

Meditation

The moral code in our society always seems to be in a state of flux. What was sacred years ago is no longer revered as holy. What was immoral in times past is common practice in our day. What was moral is now old-fashioned. Isaiah's verses in today's reading seem as appropriate for our generation as they were for the people in the prophet's time. What was evil is now looked upon as good. Being in the darkness of sin is now considered being enlightened!

We Christians are strongly tempted to adopt behaviors that are perfectly acceptable according to current cultural norms. We note many people doing things in the workplace, at school, or in the privacy of their homes that our Christian faith deems immoral. To add to our confusion, many who by Christian standards conduct themselves immorally seem to thrive.

So I wonder: Why should I be prohibited from doing such things? Why should I not conduct myself in the same manner? After all, if everyone is doing it, why should I miss out?

When I think this way, I need to remember that even though immoral behavior has become acceptable in society, it cannot be acceptable for me as a believer in Jesus Christ. I need to remember that the Lord and His teachings, and not the world's ever-changing standards, are my measure for moral behavior.

Rather than judging others, however, let me guard my own inner life and outward behavior, ensuring they are in line with the teachings of my Lord and Savior. Let me continually remove the "plank" from my own eye before I call out the "speck" in another person's eye (Matt. 7:3–5). Let me behave in a way that enlivens the Holy Spirit within my being, and by measuring the "fruit of the Spirit" growing within me (see Gal. 5:22), I will know whether or not I am on the correct moral path.

Font of Wisdom

The Little Russian Philokalia, which contains the guidance of St. Seraphim of Sarov, touches on a monumental spiritual task: discerning God's will. How does one know if thoughts or impulses received during meditation and prayer are coming from God? Saint Seraphim quotes two desert-dwelling ascetics who offered their wisdom in this regard:

> *St. Macarius of Egypt says: "Though satan might produce also visions of light, he is entirely unable to produce a blessed effect: which is the well-known sign of his works". . . And thus, from these diverse workings of the heart a man may know what is Divine and what diabolic, as St. Gregory the Sinaite writes: "From the effect one may know whether the light shining in one's soul is of God or of satan."*

The Bible warns that Satan is able to transform himself "into an angel of light" (2 Cor. 11:14). By observing whether or not the spiritual fruits of love, joy, peace, longsuffering, kindness, goodness, and faithfulness are being produced in one's heart (see Gal. 5:22), one can discern the voice of God.

REFLECTION: *On my Lenten sojourn, let me begin to discern light from darkness as I listen for the Spirit's still, small voice and perceive either peace or agitation in my heart.*

Hymn from Vespers

Let us keep a spiritual fast. Let us speak no lies or deceit with our tongue. Let us not give each other cause for stumbling, but by repentance let the lamp of our soul shine brightly. Lord, forgive us our sins.

Theophan the Recluse, Bishop of Tambov

Theophan the Recluse was born in 1815. From his youth he was interested in the monastic life of the Kievan Caves. He became a priestmonk after studying at the Kiev Theological Academy. Travels to the Holy Land inspired him to study the Church Fathers, and in his early career within the Church, he was a teacher.

Theophan had a short tenure as a bishop, during which he preached powerful sermons, but he soon resigned from his episcopal position in order to enter a monastery. A few years later he withdrew into his cell and no longer saw visitors. However, from his cell, he guided people by correspondence, and, in so doing, he left a wealth of religious and philosophical teachings, many of which are thoroughly practical today. He was considered a *staretz*, that is, an elder or experienced, inspired teacher.

Importantly, Theophan took the lead in the Russian translation of the *Philokalia*, the great treasury of Orthodox spiritual wisdom. He also adapted and edited a classic originally authored by the Western spiritual writer Lorenzo Scupoli, *Spiritual Combat*, which had been translated by Nicodemus of the Holy Mountain under the title *Unseen Warfare*.

Theophan died in his cell in 1894, at age seventy-nine. He was canonized in 1988.

PRAYER: *Help me, Lord, to devote my life to You, even though I am in the midst of this world doing ordinary and routine things each day.*

THURSDAY   Second Week of Great Lent

Meditation

The Prophet Isaiah's sixth chapter describes his awesome vision of the Kingdom of God and the Lord's throne of majesty. What is equally moving and enlightening is Isaiah's response to this revelation: "Woe *is* me, for I am undone! Because I *am* a man of unclean lips" (v. 5). His words remind me that every person in the Bible who has seen a vision of God has had a similar response.

I recall the Apostle Peter, who after seeing a miracle of Jesus responded, "Depart from me, for I am a sinful man, O Lord!" (Luke 5:8). I think of the publican, who could not lift his face before the Lord's earthly throne in the Jerusalem temple (see Luke 18:13). I remember Moses, who hid his face before the burning bush (see Ex. 3:6). I remember how the Apostles Peter, James, and John fell on their faces when Christ was transfigured before them (see Matt. 17:6).

Again and again, Scripture reveals how common people are humbled by God's presence. Their encounters bring them to their knees. Their visions make them aware of their utter sinfulness and unworthiness.

I think of how often I have entered the church, prayed my prayers, asked God for many gifts, received His precious Body and Blood, and entered the confessional with a proud, self-assured, and self-confident heart—lacking even one ounce of repentance. In that spirit, I have received nothing from the Lord's hand, while all those whom I have read about in Scripture received at least His blessing.

Font of Wisdom

Lorenzo Scupoli, a sixteenth-century Venetian priest, wrote a popular book titled *The Spiritual Combat*. This Western classic caught the attention of Nicodemus of the Holy Mountain (1749–1809), who translated the book for Eastern Christians under the title *Unseen Warfare*. Theophan the Recluse (1815–94) subsequently prepared a later edition of that work.

These saintly writers aptly describe the sin of pride, which so many Christians experience:

Since we value and think of ourselves so highly, we naturally look at others from on high [as if from a judgment seat], judge and despise them, for we seem to ourselves far removed from such faults as we think others possess.

According to this spiritual classic, the interplay between self-love and condemnation of others becomes inextricably habitual, for one fuels the other. Such unending interplay opens the door to the evil one, who craftily suggests, these authors say, that we need to "keep a sharp watch for what others say and do."

REFLECTION: *My focus on others' faults simultaneously feeds my ego and prevents me from correcting my own sins. Let me enter the labyrinth of my own thoughts and feelings to make necessary corrections.*

Hymn from Matins

If we set our hands to doing good, the effort of Lent will be a time of repentance for us, a means to eternal life. For nothing quite saves the soul as much as giving to those in need. Let us all embrace the fast.

Venerable Macrina

COMMEMORATED JULY 19/AUGUST 1

Macrina came from a saintly family. She was the eldest of the ten children of St. Basil the Elder and St. Emmelia. She was born in 327 in Caesarea, the capital of Cappadocia. Betrothed when she was merely twelve years old, Macrina was grief stricken by the sudden death of her young fiancé. She refused all other suitors and found peace only within the Church.

Macrina was a devout woman for whom the Wisdom of Solomon and the Psalms were constant companions. What she learned in her Christian journey she passed on to her siblings. Through her counsel, constant prayers, and unending admonishments, her brothers Basil (the Great), Peter (of Sebaste), and Gregory (of Nyssa) all achieved sainthood. To Basil, a proud and well-educated theologian, she taught humility. To Peter, she was a "father, mother, teacher, guide, and giver of good advice." To Gregory, she revealed joy and cheer even in the face of her own death.

Eventually, Macrina founded a monastery and became its abbess; there she guided the sisters and was recognized as a wonderworker. She died in 380, after a final prayer of thanks to the Lord for having received His blessings over the course of her life.

PRAYER: *Lord, in your Kingdom You gave Macrina equal honor with her famous brothers. Help me not to feel inferior because of lack of earthly accomplishments but to recognize the value of daily faithfulness to You.*

FRIDAY   Second Week of Great Lent

SCRIPTURE READING: PROVERBS 6:3—7:1

Meditation

It is hard to imagine that our God, who is absolute love, would hate anything. Yet yesterday's and today's readings from Proverbs clearly reveal God *does* hate not just one thing but several things!

The sixth chapter of the Book of Proverbs lists seven things *abominable* to God:

A proud look,
A lying tongue,
Hands that shed innocent blood,
A heart that devises wicked plans,
Feet that are swift in running to evil,
A false witness *who* speaks lies,
And one who sows discord among brethren (vv. 17–19).

And today's reading from the same book sternly warns against adulterous behavior, describing its destructive consequences.

Why does God hate all these things? Because each is contrary to love and, therefore, contrary to Him.

In all honesty I can admit there isn't one of these seven things I have not either committed or wanted to commit! To one degree or another, consciously or unconsciously, openly or secretly, out of retaliation or out of boredom, I've willingly engaged in them all. (As far as shedding innocent blood is concerned, remember the words of the Apostle John: "Whoever hates his brother is a murderer, and you know that no murderer has eternal life abiding in him" [1 John 3:15]. And as far as adultery is concerned, remember Jesus' words about lustful eyes [Matt. 5:28].)

Each time I engage in such abominable ways, I recognize I have offended my God. How glad I am that God hates the things I do, but does not hate me! By experiencing His love I am motivated to stop hurting Him and to repent of my sinful ways.

Font of Wisdom

The Eastern spiritual classic *Unseen Warfare* expertly unwinds the origins of sinful thoughts and behavior while offering remedies for healing of the soul. A particularly stinging passage reads:

> *Moreover, when you judge severely some wrong action of your neighbour, you must know that a small root of the same wickedness is also in our own heart, which, by its passionate nature, teaches you to make suppositions about others and to judge them.*

Having identified the root cause of a severely judgmental nature, the author of the book offers a two-pronged cure: first, replace the critical thoughts about others with thoughts about their good qualities, and second, be constantly aware of your own unworthiness.

REFLECTION: *Will I admit to this spiritual axiom: After I have severely judged another person, I suddenly remember an occasion on which I too have acted similarly.*

Hymn from Vespers

Now is the acceptable time, now is the day of salvation. In the abundance of Your mercy visit my soul and take away the burden of my sins, O only Lover of humankind.

Patrick, Bishop of Armagh, Enlightener of Ireland

Patrick, born about 386, was of Romano-British origin. Though not a strong believer while growing up in Wales, he radically increased his faith when in his early teens pirates carried him off to Ireland.

During his six-year enslavement in Ireland, Patrick labored as a swineherd. Day and night he prayed fervently to be set free and to be reunited with his family. In answer to his prayer, a voice in a dream bade him to seek out a ship in a harbor two hundred miles away, which would take him back home. That night he ran away from his masters, ultimately boarded the ship, and shortly thereafter reunited with his family.

Patrick spent the next years preparing for ordination to the priesthood. He spent much of his time in France, where he met Bishop Germanus, who later consecrated Patrick as bishop of Ireland.

Upon his return to Ireland, a land dominated by pagan worship and magicians, Patrick countered their false teachings with great signs and preaching. In humility and simplicity he used plain language and homely examples to explain the Faith, and he became recognized as an effective preacher and teacher. His use of the shamrock, or three-leaf clover, to explain the nature and Persons of the Holy Trinity is famous among his many illustrations.

Patrick ascribed all his success in spreading the gospel to God, saying, "I owe it to God's grace that through me so many people should be born again to Him." By the time he established the episcopal see in Armagh in 444, Patrick had several clergy assisting him. He reposed in 461.

PRAYER: *Open my mind, Lord, to hear and understand those who have knowledge of You.*

SATURDAY   Second Week of Great Lent

SCRIPTURE READING: MARK 1:35–44

Meditation

Time and again, as in today's reading, Jesus prohibits those He cures from spreading the good news of their healing. Most often, they do not heed His command, and then thousands more from that same locale come for His blessing.

It is not out of mere modesty that Jesus tries to dissuade those He heals from spreading the word about Him. Rather, He wants to avoid being associated with sensationalism. He has come to save humankind, not just to perform miracles that effect bodily healing. He has come to call people to repentance, to a change of heart, to a turning back to God. But, according to the Gospels, many in the crowds that follow Him just don't get it.

Sometimes I wonder if *I* get it. I often want God only when I am in need or in pain, or suffering. I want things from Him, rather than wanting just Him. Worse, when I do not receive what I want when I want it, I turn away from Him in the blink of an eye. This is not the kind of relationship with me Christ desires, so the leper in today's Gospel can teach me a valuable lesson.

Christ heals the leper because the man is willing to accept Christ's *will*. He does not say, "You must heal me because You are a miracle worker." He says, "If You are willing, You can make me clean" (Mark 1:40). Isn't this what I pray daily in the Lord's Prayer: "Your will be done"? May I begin to heed this type of prayer in true faith.

Font of Wisdom

The dilemma of unanswered prayer mystifies many Christians. Saint Isaac the Syrian (613–c. 700), quoting the *Praktikos* of Evagrius Ponticus (346–99), provides insight as to why God may not answer a prayer in the way a supplicant wishes:

> *If you should beseech God for a thing and He is slow to hearken to you speedily, do not grieve, for you are not wiser than God. This happens to you either because you are not worthy to obtain your request, or because the pathways of your heart do not accord with your petitions (but rather the contrary), or because you have not yet reached the measure wherein you could receive the gift you ask for.*

Saint Isaac reminds his readers their Father in Heaven knows all their true needs (Matt. 6:32), and He acts out of wisdom and love; therefore they should not despair if their prayers go unanswered. He also observes that human beings are most grateful for answered prayer only *after* an internal struggle. "For anything that is quickly obtained is also easily lost," he notes, "whereas everything found with toil is also kept with careful watching."

REFLECTION: *Let me stay faithful to God and trust in His wisdom, even when my prayers either are not answered immediately or are not answered in accordance with my wishes.*

Hymn from Vespers

Your tongue, watchful in teaching, rings in the ears of our hearts and awakens the souls of the slothful. Your words are inspired by God. . . . O Gregory of Thessalonica, do not cease to pray before Christ our God.

Cyril, Archbishop of Jerusalem

Saint Cyril, a gentle man during turbulent times, was born around 315, most likely in Jerusalem. The son of Christian parents, he received a fine education, and he had a superior command of Holy Scripture.

He was ordained as a priest by Bishop Maximos of Jerusalem, who thought so highly of Cyril's abilities that he placed him in charge of instructing the catechumens—that is, those who were preparing for baptism. Cyril's talks titled *Catechetical Lectures on the Sacraments* would become treasured classics. They contain detailed instructions about fourth-century liturgical rites within the Church's worship.

Upon becoming the archbishop of the city of Jerusalem, Cyril found himself at odds with Acacius, one of the bishops who had consecrated him. Acacius was an Arian—he believed Jesus Christ was created by God, like any other human being. Cyril, in defending the traditional dogma that Christ was uncreated, took the brunt of Acacius's wrath. Acacius and his fellow Arians accused Cyril of selling church property during a severe famine and giving the proceeds to the poor—a well-founded charge that led to Cyril's exile. The godly bishop was exiled three times during his episcopacy, a punishment totaling sixteen years.

Throughout his maltreatment, Cyril remained steadfast in his faith and in his declaration of Orthodox teaching. He died around 386 after serving thirty-five years as a bishop.

PRAYER: *Grant me, O Lord, the spirit of gentleness.*

SUNDAY   Second Week of Great Lent
Sunday of Saint Gregory Palamas
SCRIPTURE READING: MARK 2:1–12

Meditation

On the second Sunday of Great Lent we hear the story of the paralytic who was borne on a pallet by his friends and laid at the feet of Jesus. We also read of Jesus revealing His Divinity as He grants forgiveness to the paralytic and heals him solely by the power of His word.

This Gospel account nudges me to consider the power of friendship. I'm astounded by the outrageous and determined act of the four men; they bypass pressing crowds, strip open a roof, and lower their helpless companion directly in front of the Lord!

Friendship is a give-and-take relationship, usually balanced, usually reciprocal. But I wonder what the paralytic, given his limitations, had to offer those four men in return for their friendship?

Equally, I ponder the reciprocity of my own friendships. Admittedly, I feel safer when I am the one who gives more to a friendship, though I have been grateful at times to share with others my deepest fears and all-too-real weaknesses. I have found that true friends think the best of me even when they see the worst of me. Their care and support have helped me through many difficult times. Importantly, God continues to reveal His love to me *through* the love of my friends.

Jesus forgave and healed the paralytic when He saw the faith of his friends. May I be determined to develop and maintain solid, honest friendships. By so doing, I will please my Lord, who teaches me even to lay down my own life for my friends (see John 15:13).

Font of Wisdom

The Apostle Paul writes, "I beseech you therefore, brethren, by the mercies of God, that you present your bodies a living sacrifice, holy, acceptable to God, *which is* your reasonable service" (Rom. 12:1). In his work titled *The Triads*, St. Gregory Palamas (1296–1359) pens a reflection on this scripture, presenting ways to offer one's body as a "sacrifice pleasing to God":

> *Our eyes must acquire a gentle glance, attractive to others and conveying the mercy from on high. . . . Similarly, our ears must be attentive to the divine instructions, not only to hear them, but (as David says) "to remember the commandments of God . . . in order to perform them." . . . Our tongues, our hands and feet must likewise be at the service of the Divine Will.*

Saint Gregory further urges fellow Christians, saying, "Is not such a practice of the commandments of God a common activity of body and soul?"

REFLECTION: *As I continue my Lenten journey, let me not only tend the interior garden of my soul but also offer my body in service to God.*

Hymn from the Divine Liturgy

O light of Orthodoxy, teacher of the Church, its confirmation; O ideal of monks and invincible champion of theologians; O wonder-working Gregory, glory of Thessalonica and preacher of grace; always intercede before the Lord that our souls may be saved.

Gregory Palamas, Archbishop of Thessalonica

Gregory Palamas was born in the year 1296 and was educated in Constantinople. He became a monk and spent much of his life on Mount Athos. He was ordained a priest at age thirty.

Gregory practiced *hesychasm*—a mystical life of silence, rigorous bodily discipline and fasting, and the continuous repetition of the Jesus Prayer: "Lord, Jesus Christ, Son of God, be merciful to me, a sinner." Through this method of prayer, "hesychasts," as they were called, were often granted spiritual grace. Palamas himself balanced his personal and communal prayer by attending Divine Liturgy and receiving the sacraments at his monastery on Saturdays and Sundays.

Gregory became the main defender of hesychasm when a controversy led by the philosopher Barlaam broke out. Barlaam denied the idea that human beings could experience genuine union with God. Refining the argument, Gregory made a distinction between the essence of God, which is unknowable, and the divine energies of God, which can be shared with human beings. The debate over hesychastic practice went on for more than twenty years, but Gregory's position eventually received recognition and approval by the Church.

Gregory, who also had become archbishop of Thessalonica in 1347, earned respect as a pastor and teacher. He was canonized in 1368, just nine years after his death, and he has earned renown as one of the foremost apologists for the Orthodox Faith.

PRAYER: *Lord, guide me in finding the proper balance between personal prayer and prayer within the community of the Church.*

SCRIPTURE READING: GENESIS 6:9–22

Meditation

In many Old Testament stories, God's communication to human beings rings loud and clear. He gives certain people specific instructions requiring concrete actions. The recipients of His Word know it is God who speaks, and they understand exactly what He directs them to do.

In today's scripture, God tells Noah to build an ark, giving him clear directions as to its length, width, height, and even type of wood. Then He tells Noah how to fill up the vessel and when to board the ark. Noah, being faithful and obedient—even in the face of ridicule—does exactly what God tells him, without questioning the Lord.

If God told me to build an ark and gather animals, I would no doubt argue with Him. I might protest: "I live on a hill." "It doesn't flood often in this area." "Why do you want me to do this?"

At times I do pray sincerely for direction and guidance, for I know my tendency to make wrong decisions and to choose wrong paths. I admit I need God's help, and I desire the clarity of His presence. But simultaneously, I find it difficult to be still in my heart and to wait for God to speak to me. Many times I want God simply to affirm what I have already concluded!

I know also that God can speak to me through Scripture whenever I lack the peace or calm necessary to hear His voice in prayer. Even then, however, I retort: "I can't do that." "What if I fail?" "It's too hard." "It doesn't seem necessary." "Isn't there an easier way?"

Let me look to Noah as my faithful example—obedient, with complete trust in God. Let me overcome the chasm in my mind and in my will between doubtful questioning and confident obedience.

Font of Wisdom

In his work *The Discourses*, St. Symeon the New Theologian (949–1022) describes the brilliant radiance of God, as well as his personal encounter with the Divinity. Symeon claims God became visible to him when, through the Holy Spirit, He entirely cleansed his mind.

In astonishment and trembling, St. Symeon queried this Being: "O Master, who art Thou?" Then he recalls how gently God answered:

> *I am God who have become man for your sake. Because you have sought me with all your soul, behold, from now on you will be My brother . . . My fellow heir . . . and My friend.*

REFLECTION: *In my striving for goodness, I often forget about the gentle side of God. Will I take time to think of Him as my friend who lovingly accompanies me on my pilgrimage?*

Hymn from Matins

I am clothed in the foul filth of my transgressions. I have been driven from the chamber of joy. But be bountiful to me through Your ineffable compassion as You were to the Prodigal Son, O God, and have mercy on me.

Martyr Photina, the Samaritan Woman

COMMEMORATED FEBRUARY 26/MARCH 10

The Gospel of John 4:5–42 tells of an encounter between Jesus and a Samaritan woman who has come to draw water from Jacob's Well. At first Jesus, being wearied from His journey, asks her to draw water for Him to drink. Then, during their startling conversation, He offers her "a fountain of water springing up into everlasting life" (v. 14).

Jesus' words puzzle her, but she, hoping to ease her burden of daily hauling water from the well, asks for this miraculous drink. Once she recognizes Jesus as the promised Messiah, she spreads the word to her fellow citizens; many of them go out to meet and speak with Jesus, and they also come to believe in Him as the Savior of the world. In proclaiming Jesus, the Samaritan woman turns away from her less-than-savory lifestyle and becomes an evangelist.

After Jesus' Resurrection and the outpouring of the Holy Spirit on Pentecost (Acts 2), this woman was baptized, taking the new name of *Photina*, meaning "light" or "the enlightened one." Photina and some of her children were then sent to Carthage by the apostles to spread the gospel. Her son Victor converted the Duke of Italy, Sebastian (later canonized), to the Christian Faith.

Emperor Nero, who encouraged the persecution of Christians, had Photina, her children, and other Christians associated with them imprisoned. While she was jailed, however, Photina converted and baptized Nero's daughter Domnina and one hundred of her servants! This news further enraged Nero, and he condemned Photina and her company of Christians to heinous tortures: flaying of skin, cutting off limbs, beheading, and even tearing one of Photina's companions in two. Photina herself was thrown down a well, where she surrendered her soul to God in the year 66.

PRAYER: *Enlighten my life, Lord, with Your holy light, and let my life be a light rather than a hindrance to others.*

TUESDAY   Third Week of Great Lent

SCRIPTURE READING: PROVERBS 8:32—9:11

Meditation

When I read the familiar verses from the Book of Proverbs, "The fear of the LORD *is* the beginning of wisdom, / And the knowledge of the Holy One *is* understanding" (Prov. 9:10), I need to define "fear" as a sense of awe. When I regard the Lord God with reverence, I begin to grow in discernment.

It is difficult to keep an awesome God uppermost in my mind as I direct my attention to many other things that I value and revere: mutual love of family and friends, physical and mental abilities, social status and possessions. I am thankful for these wonderful blessings, which provide not only for my own welfare but also for the welfare of others.

Still, I must keep foremost in mind God's majesty, offering my life to Him and letting Him sanctify me in return. When I cease to hold the Lord in awe, I begin to view my blessings from God as gods in themselves; I begin to use my relationships and possessions selfishly, instead of offering them up for His glory.

When I stop reverencing God, I become the center of my world. Then my life loses focus and my thinking becomes scattered. But when I am awestruck by everything He is and everything He does and all that He gives me, I engage in life with renewed purpose and clarity of thought.

Font of Wisdom

Father John of Kronstadt (1829–1909), pastor par excellence at St. Andrew's Cathedral in the naval base city of Kronstadt, near St. Petersburg, Russia, was revered for his powerful prayer. In his work *My Life in Christ* he explains why prayer is essential to the spiritual life:

> Our heart dies spiritually every day. Only ardent, tearful prayer can restore it to breath and life. If we do not pray fervently every day we may easily and speedily be overtaken by spiritual death.

Just as it is necessary, he says, to eat, drink, and exercise daily in order to strengthen, support, and cleanse the body, likewise it is necessary to pray daily in order to strengthen, support, and cleanse the soul. "The only means by which you can spend the day in perfect holiness, and peace, and without sin, is most sincere prayer as soon as you rise from sleep in the morning," he teaches. "It will bring Christ into your heart, with the Father and the Holy Ghost."

REFLECTION: *I dedicate much time to the care of my body but devote little time to my withering soul. Let me enliven my heart by saying often during the day, "Lord, Jesus Christ, Son of God, be merciful to me, a sinner," or at least, "Lord, have mercy."*

Hymn from Vespers

By enlightening our souls through fasting, O Lord, may we be enabled to behold Your Cross in joy—in fear to bow before it. The Cross illumines Your voluntary sufferings. Grant us to behold them, O Lover of humanity.

Great-martyr Barbara

In early Christianity within the Roman Empire, believers were seen as threats to established religious and social norms. They were labeled as subversive and seditious because of their refusal to sacrifice to pagan idols, which represented imperial power and order.

Saint Barbara lived at the end of the third century in Heliopolis, where her wealthy father, Dioscorus, was the governor. The extraordinarily beautiful young woman was disciplined, educated, polite, and modest. As she matured, she came to view the pagan idols as soulless, and she sought with all her heart to discover the Creator of the beautiful world surrounding her. She decided to dedicate herself to this pursuit, and she vowed to remain a virgin.

Her father, wishing to protect her from unwanted overtures by many suitors, secluded Barbara in a tower. However, when the time came for her to marry, she refused the many nobles who asked Dioscorus for her hand. Dioscorus, assuming Barbara's mind had been negatively affected by her life of seclusion, began to allow her to socialize more freely. During that time Barbara discovered the One True God, secretly became a Christian, and received Holy Baptism.

When Dioscorus built a new bathhouse for Barbara, she had three windows installed in honor of the Holy Trinity—instead of the original two called for in the architectural plans. Her father was infuriated when she told him the reason for the change. Unable to persuade her to give up her newfound faith, he himself beat her, handed her over for torture in front of jeering crowds, and finally murdered her by his own hand through beheading.

PRAYER: *Saint Barbara desired only the joy of serving you. Lord, help me to know that You are the true source of my joy and the true Creator of all that is beautiful.*

SCRIPTURE READING: PROVERBS 9:12–18

Meditation

Today's reading from the Book of Proverbs clearly shows us the power of sin. Sin, appearing attractive, lures us and fools us into engaging in it.

God Himself does not tempt me, but He does allow me to be tempted by my own sinful desires and passions. Why? Because through resisting temptation I learn humility and patience. Through struggling with temptation I grow spiritually. Through fighting temptation I win victory by the Cross. The fire of spiritual warfare purifies my faith and love.

Besides warning me about the lure of sin, Scripture also warns me against entrapment by sin. Entrapment occurs when I've failed in fighting a temptation and have invited sin into my life, whether in thought or in action. In the Gospel of John, Jesus says, "Most assuredly, I say to you, whoever commits sin is a slave of sin" (8:34). Just as a slave would find it nearly impossible to escape from a master, I find it difficult to escape from my habitual sins and my regular indulgence in them.

Yet God offers me solutions to temptation and entrapment. Saint Paul says in Romans 6:23, "For the wages of sin *is* death, but the gift of God *is* eternal life in Christ Jesus our Lord."

I certainly have experienced my sins causing the death of the Spirit of God in my soul. However, God continues to encourage me in my vigilance and strengthen me in my weakness while offering me opportunities to repent. With thankfulness, I recall other words of St. Paul, "O Death, where *is* your sting? / O Hades, where *is* your victory?" (1 Cor. 15:55).

Font of Wisdom

Saint Tikhon of Zadonsk (1724–83) served Christ not only as bishop of the vast diocese of Voronezh in Russia but also as abbot of a monastery and rector of a seminary during his lifetime. His advice regarding sins of the tongue is preserved in writing and offers tough but sage words regarding the ubiquitous human foible of gossiping:

If you see or hear someone sin, keep from slandering him and judging him. You tell someone else about him, he tells it to another, the other to the third, the third to the fourth, and so everyone will come to know it and be tempted. And they will judge the one who sinned, which is a very serious thing. And you will be the cause of all this, by publishing your brother's sin. Slanderers are like lepers that harm others by their foul odor, or like those stricken by the plague who carry their disease from place to place and destroy others. . . . A righteous man has no need to judge and condemn another, how much less should a sinner judge a sinner.

REFLECTION: *The Prayer of St. Ephraim—which I repeat frequently during Great Lent—reminds me "not to judge my brother" (or sister) and to abstain from "idle talk." Am I merely parroting the words of that prayer, or am I putting them into practice?*

Hymn from the Presanctified Liturgy

O martyrs of the Lord, living sacrifices, spiritual oblations, perfect victims, sheep who know God and are known by Him, pray that we too may graze with you beside still waters.

Nicholas, Equal to the Apostles, Enlightener of Japan

Ivan Kasatkin was born in 1836 in the diocese of Smolensk, Russia. After studying at St. Petersburg Theological Academy, he felt called to do missionary work, so he volunteered to serve as priest of the Russian Consulate in Hakodate, Japan. After taking monastic vows and the name Nicholas, he arrived in Japan in 1861, at a time when—according to Nicholas's own account—Japan looked upon "foreigners as beasts" and Christians as a "villainous sect."

Happily, Hieromonk Nicholas was inspired by a lengthy meeting in Siberia with the great missionary to Alaska, Archbishop Innocent (later canonized). Their deep conversations proved to have a long-lasting influence on the Church in Japan. Father Nicholas began zealously to study the language and culture of the Japanese. Just as Archbishop Innocent had done for the Aleut people in North America, Hieromonk Nicholas translated the Scripture and service books into the vernacular. He also trained native Japanese to be church workers, published religious materials for their use, and worked to improve their quality of life. By the year 1878, there were about four thousand Orthodox Christians in Japan.

Father Nicholas established a seminary and was elevated to the rank of bishop. He consecrated the Holy Resurrection Cathedral in Tokyo in 1891. After he and his flock endured the hardships of the Russo-Japanese War, he was elevated to the rank of archbishop. At the time of the fiftieth anniversary of his priesthood in 1911, there were thirty thousand Orthodox Christians in Japan. In 1912, he peacefully reposed in the Lord. The Holy Synod of the Russian Orthodox Church glorified him in 1970.

PRAYER: *When there is an obstacle in my path, it is so easy to simply stop. Help me, Lord, to persevere in overcoming the obstacles in my relationships with You and with my sisters and brothers.*

THURSDAY   Third Week of Great Lent

Meditation

I admit that I sin before God, but I run into barriers when I want to confess my sins in the Sacrament of Confession. Either I consider some sins to be so trivial that I brush them aside, or I consider them to be so great that I cannot forgive myself.

Thus, I become my own god. By minimizing my sin, I usurp God's judgment. By refusing to forgive myself, I assume His place as Forgiver—doubting His mercy and ignoring His salvific work on the Cross. Both my nonchalance and my self-condemnation isolate me from His forgiveness.

When either of these two things occurs, I must admit that the impossibility of my reconciliation with Him is a problem that lies within *me*. Then I must take the first step: I need to come before God and express my dilemma regarding my attitude toward my sins. He will then help me take the next step toward reconciliation and inner healing.

God is always ready to forgive me and to offer me His peace. He is waiting until I come to Him in repentance, with a true desire to change the state of my heart and the direction of my life. My sins are never too great or too many for Him to forgive.

In today's reading from the Prophet Isaiah, I see how God has been angry with His people, but now He gathers them together. He draws them back to Himself with hope and promise. When I accept His forgiveness and reconciliation, I too can sing with His people,

For YAH, the LORD, is my strength and song;
He also has become my salvation. (12:2)

Font of Wisdom

Saint Theophan the Recluse (1815–94), bishop of Rostov, wrote much about the practice of interior prayer. Some of his writings on prayer have appeared in *The Art of Prayer* and in *Russian Mystics*.

Saint Theophan's guidance includes praying secretly to God in one's heart *continually*. The Lord Himself, he claims, has commanded all Christians without exception to do so (Matt. 6:6), as has the Apostle Paul (Eph. 6:18). He writes:

> To pray unceasingly is possible only in the heart. Therefore it is impossible to contest the fact that mental prayer is compulsory for all Christians, and if it is obligatory it is also possible—God does not command the impossible.

REFLECTION: *Let me ask my Savior to help me commune in my heart with Him constantly. I can only imagine the joy of walking with Him every moment.*

Hymn from Vespers

We have completed the third week of the fast. Enable us, O Christ, to behold the wood of Your lifebearing Cross: to bow before it worthily, to praise and glorify Your majesty, to exalt and magnify Your Passion, to attain in purity the holy, glorious Resurrection through which Adam re-enters Paradise—the mystical Pascha.

Martyr Nikon and 199 Disciples in Sicily

As a youth in Italy in the third century, Nikon showed military talent, so he joined the Roman army and became a topnotch soldier. His skill earned him a long leave, which he chose to spend in the city of Byzantium. En route his ship anchored at a Greek island for repair, and Nikon disembarked. While ashore, he met a holy man whose talk of Jesus Christ and the Church so impressed him that he missed his ship's sailing. This mattered little to Nikon, who by now had become convinced his life was to be spent serving Christ. He first was tonsured a monk and after three years was ordained a priest.

Later he became a bishop and was sent to a large Sicilian monastery. He is described in literature about the saints (hagiography) as a holy ascetic, and the 199 monks who lived and ministered with him were pious and dedicated. The monastery became a retreat center, a source of inspiration and an aid to its surrounding community.

Initially civil authorities near this monastic center considered the monks to be harmless recluses, but the local governor became concerned that his power was being undermined by their Christian faith. He ordered Nikon either to abandon the monastery or to face martyrdom. Nikon and his monks chose the latter. On March 23, 251, Nikon was forced to watch as each of his fellow monks was slaughtered. Then he too was martyred.

PRAYER: *When I struggle in my relationship with You, Lord, let me remember the times You have filled me with the warmth of Your love.*

SCRIPTURE READING: PROVERBS 10:31—11:12

Meditation

One of Christianity's many blessings is the sense of community developed with others through unity in our Lord. God calls us to be brothers and sisters, for He has adopted us as sons and daughters through the death and Resurrection of His only-begotten Son and His gift of the Holy Spirit (Gal. 4:4–7).

As in any family, difficulties arise in relationships within the Church, but the Lord teaches us proper ways to deal with them. Matthew 18:15 instructs the Christian community how to heal a broken relationship: discuss the difficulty privately with the one who has hurt you; only when your attempt to mend the relationship fails should you bring others in to resolve the problem.

In today's lesson from Proverbs, several verses remind me of the importance of speaking with care. Pointing out another person's sins privately in a loving manner is an act of kindness; pointing them out publicly with the intent of belittling another person is an act of perversion.

Throughout Great Lent, I say the prayer of St. Ephraim of Syria, "Grant me to see my own sins and not to judge my brother. . . ." If I truly felt this prayer, I would not judge my brothers and sisters readily. If I had the spirit of humility, I would not need to build myself up by tearing them down. My misplaced pride persuades me that I will appear superior if others around me appear inferior. I need to heal relationships, not destroy them.

Font of Wisdom

Nowadays fasting is fashionable! Medical researchers tout its health benefits based on scientific evidence. Interestingly, St. John of

Kronstadt (1829–1909), in his work *My Life in Christ*, also recommends fasting to Christians. "Fasting," he says, "is a good teacher" for several reasons:

> (1) It soon makes everybody who fasts understand that a man needs very little food and drink, and that in general we are greedy and eat a great deal more than is necessary. (2) Fasting clearly discloses all the sins and defects, all the weaknesses and diseases of our soul, just as when one begins to clean out muddy, stagnant water the reptiles and dirt that lurk in it are revealed. (3) It shows us the necessity of turning to God with the whole heart, and of seeking his mercy, help and saving grace. (4) Fasting shows us all the craftiness, cunning and malice of the bodiless spirits, whom we have hitherto unwittingly served, and who now malignantly persecute us for having ceased to follow them.

Saint John reminds his readers that no matter what healthy foods they eat or what healthy exercise they engage in to preserve their bodies, they will nevertheless end up in a grave. He urges Christians to fast for one purpose: to set their eyes on the Kingdom of God, which is "not eating and drinking, but righteousness and peace and joy in the Holy Spirit" (Rom. 14:17).

REFLECTION: *Do I view fasting either as a legalistic discipline or as a health benefit, rather than as a means to lead my spirit and body toward the Kingdom of God?*

Hymn from Presanctified Liturgy

I turned away from Your grace like the Prodigal. I wasted the riches of Your kindness, O Lord. Now I run to You and cry: I have sinned, O God, have mercy.

Venerable Simeon the Stylite, the Elder

From his youth, Simeon, a shepherd's son born around the year 390, lived in monasteries and hermitages in northern Syria and practiced ever-increasing austerities. He chose a life of deprivation, especially in fasting; during the forty days of Great Lent, he was able to abstain from food and drink. Because of his holiness, people began to come to Simeon for his advice and blessing. These distractions interrupted his solitude, so in 420 he initiated a unique lifestyle: he erected a pillar on which to dwell. The pillar—about 6 feet high with an 11-square-foot platform—had no seat and offered little opportunity for Simeon to rest between his many prostrations during prayer.

At first neighboring bishops considered his behavior excessive, and they ordered him to come down from his perch. Because Simeon obeyed his hierarchs in humility, he was permitted to continue his singular lifestyle. Thus he earned the name *stylite*, which derives from the Greek word for "pillar." Simeon dwelt for thirty-seven years on such columns, which he built successively higher.

Simeon's holiness lay not only in his extraordinary lifestyle but also in his charity, patience, and humility. He spoke daily to crowds gathering near him, and his messages were practical and full of common sense. He earned great respect and converted many to belief in the Lord. He spent his last twenty years on a pillar 65 feet high. Simeon reposed in 459.

PRAYER: *Although I may appear odd in practicing my Christian faith amid the enticements of the world, I do not want to be separated from You, Lord. Help me to rise above my fears.*

SATURDAY   Third Week of Great Lent

Meditation

Jesus commanded Matthew (Levi) in today's reading by saying "Follow Me" (Mark 2:14). Likewise, He calls all of us. Perhaps we have not had as dramatic a personal encounter with Jesus as Matthew did, but certainly we have heard Him call to us—perhaps through reading Scripture, perhaps through a friend's voice, perhaps by a still, small voice speaking in our heart.

In response to His call, I've often proclaimed Jesus Christ as my Lord and God. I've even professed a desire to follow Him whole-heartedly. But the truth is, despite my intentions, I have yet to surrender myself fully to Him. I'm tentative about bending to His will.

There's a reason for this. When I do draw near to Him, His call seems to grow more insistent, and His way seems to become more difficult. My good intentions repeatedly fall by the wayside as I choose between surrendering my will to Him and pursuing my own desires. So I retreat, hastily following any other path than the way He is indicating. Intellectually I know that Jesus Christ is ultimately responsible for what I am and what I possess, but when I consider giving myself fully to Him, I instead turn away from Him—and His call—and my ears grow dull.

Worse, while claiming to follow Jesus, I actually desire *independence* from Him. I take pleasure in feeling superior, more righteous, more deserving than others. Like the Pharisee in the Gospel (Luke 18:9–14), I judge others with a hard heart.

Thankfully, Jesus continues to issue His call, no matter my inner state. He calls me to repentance; He calls me to eat and drink of Himself in Holy Communion; He calls me to the healing of my spirit, soul, and body. The Great Physician calls me to an unceasing struggle, leading to my cleansing, forgiveness, and union with Him.

Font of Wisdom

Theophan the Recluse (1815–94), a monastic saint, wrote four homilies as well as several articles on prayer. He distinguishes between external prayer, which consists simply in verbal expression and form, and internal prayer, which is a spiritual turning toward God:

> *What then is prayer? Prayer is the raising of the mind and heart to God in praise and thanksgiving to Him and in supplication for the good things that we need, both spiritual and physical. The essence of prayer is therefore the spiritual lifting of the heart towards God. The mind in the heart stands consciously before the face of God, filled with due reverence, and begins to pour itself out before Him. This is spiritual prayer, and all prayer should be of this nature.*

REFLECTION: *Let me harness my scattered thoughts and focus inward (where my soul's emotions and passions reside) before turning my entire being to God in prayer—face to face and heart to heart.*

Hymn from Vespers

Shine, O Cross of the Lord! Illumine the hearts of those who honor you. With love inspired by God we embrace you, the only hope of the world. Through you our tears are wiped away. . . . We pass over into everlasting joy. Help us who ask for mercy in faith.

Gregory the Theologian, Archbishop of Constantinople
COMMEMORATED JANUARY 25/FEBRUARY 7

Gregory the Theologian (also known as Gregory of Nazianzus), son of the saintly Nonna and Gregory the Elder, was born about 329 in Cappadocia, near the center of present-day Turkey. He received an extensive education, both in fine secular schools and from family members, who immersed his mind in the Holy Scriptures. After surviving a raging storm at sea while on his way to study in Athens, Gregory vowed to dedicate himself to God, and he was baptized at age thirty-three. From that time forward, he offered his immense literary talent to Christ and His Church.

Eventually the gentle, peace-loving Gregory was ordained not only to the priesthood but also to the episcopacy—reluctantly and against his own desires. Nevertheless, in these roles he supported not only his own father, who was bishop of Nazianzus, but also his former schoolmate, Basil, who had become the archbishop of Caesarea.

Throughout his lifetime, Gregory was called upon to fight against heretical teachings promulgated by wayward clergy and upheld by powerful rulers. His theological works—orations, poems, and letters—argued against false doctrines held by the Arians, Macedonians, Apollinarians, and Eunomians. His penetrating argumentation once led to his being severely beaten by an opposing mob while he baptized catechumens in the Church of the Resurrection in the capital city of Constantinople on Pascha night.

At the Second Ecumenical Council in 381, Gregory was chosen to be patriarch of Constantinople. He later resigned the position and retired to the solitude of Arianzus, where he continued to affirm Orthodox teachings through his writings. He died on January 25, 389, and was buried at Nazianzus. His relics were later transferred to both Constantinople and Rome. The Church honors him as "the Theologian," a title also given to the holy Apostle and Evangelist John.

PRAYER: *Thank you, Lord, for the friendships that enrich my life. May I be supportive to my friends, as St. Gregory the Theologian was to his friend, St. Basil the Great.*

SUNDAY   Third Week of Great Lent
Sunday of the Veneration of the Cross
SCRIPTURE READING: MARK 8:34—9:1

Meditation

Jesus' solemn command to deny ourselves, take up our cross, and follow Him seems extreme, even severe. Yet the Church deems it necessary for us to hear this Gospel passage annually, midway through Great Lent.

Experientially, I understand this wise decision. Each year, as I listen to this passage and kiss the beautifully decorated cross in the center of the church, I am inspired to try harder in my Lenten efforts. I become more diligent in prayer and in reading the Bible. I fast more rigorously. I do good deeds toward others in secret. I practice self-denial (for a time). Sadly, after Pascha, I usually shelve all my good intentions, without having internalized the lessons of Lent.

Why? In one word: pride. Over the years I have figured out I am afraid there will be nothing left of "me" if I do not hold on to my own self—if I let go and follow Him completely. My prideful fear places a barrier between Him and me.

I need to remember Jesus has pledged to be with me not only on my Lenten journey but also on my life's journey. In the Scriptures I read that Jesus' Transfiguration on Mount Tabor occurs soon after His message about the cross. God promises that if I lose myself for His sake and for the sake of the gospel, I will witness His glory. I will also be transformed.

Let me cling to His promise. In so doing, I will find my *true* self.

Font of Wisdom

Theophan the Recluse (1815–94), a master instructor of prayer, speaks specifically about preparation for prayer in one of his four homilies on the subject. In his first sermon, "A Personal Rule of Prayer," he insists that both "heart and mind" must absorb the content of a prayer in order for it to be edifying. He gives three simple instructions:

> First, do not start to pray without at least some brief preparation; second, do not perform your prayer carelessly, but do so with attention and feeling; third, do not return to your usual occupations immediately after you have finished praying.

Saint Theophan fleshes out these three principles, urging us to "stand awhile, sit for a while, or walk a little and try to steady your mind and turn it away from all worldly activities and objects" before beginning to pray. After this, he advises to measure mentally the gap between the supplicant and God in order to awaken "reverent awe" in the soul.

REFLECTION: *Being a creature with so little time—even for family and friends—will I take the time to pause—even for one minute—before and after praying to my Lord?*

Hymn from Divine Liturgy

O Lord, save Your people and bless Your inheritance. Grant victory to Orthodox Christians over their adversaries. And by virtue of Your Cross, preserve Your habitation.

Venerable Ephraim the Syrian
COMMEMORATED JANUARY 28/FEBRUARY 10

Ephraim was born early in the fourth century in Nisibis (now in southeastern Turkey, bordering Syria). His quick youthful temper and bad habits eventually were tamed after he became a monk under the guidance of the holy hierarch James (Jacob) of Nisibis. Ephraim devoted himself to praying, fasting, and studying Holy Scripture, living first as an ascetic in the mountains of his hometown and later as a monk in a monastery near the city of Edessa.

Recognizing Ephraim's abilities, the bishop James allowed him to preach sermons and to instruct schoolchildren. He even had Ephraim accompany him to the First Ecumenical Council in Nicea in 325, which condemned the Arian heresy—a false doctrine that denied Jesus of Nazareth was the uncreated the Word of God.

Ephraim's legacy includes several hymns and prayers sprung from the spiritual well within him. These include prayers to the Theotokos, the Holy Trinity, and the Son of God. Perhaps the best-known is the Lenten prayer that begins "O Lord and Master of my life." He also wrote a Syriac commentary on the first five books of the Bible.

Ephraim's works were amazingly popular, even during his own lifetime. Saint Jerome, the historian, attests that his works were read publicly in some churches, following the reading of Holy Scripture. Ephraim is also said to have trained female choirs to sing in public forums—using his phrasing of traditional doctrine as lyrics and employing popular folk tunes as melodies. In this way, he cleverly spread the truth of the gospel and the apostolic teaching.

Toward the end of his life, Ephraim traveled both to Egypt, to observe the ascetic labors of the desert monks, and to Caesarea, where he was ordained a deacon by Basil, archbishop of Caesarea, in 371. Ephraim refused ordination to the priesthood, claiming he was unworthy of the honor. Some accounts of his life suggest Ephraim died while ministering to victims of a plague in 373.

PRAYER: *Let my heart and lips sing to You, my Lord.*

MONDAY   Fourth Week of Great Lent

SCRIPTURE READING: PROVERBS 11:19—12:6

Meditation

Verse 24 of today's reading from Proverbs 11 says, "There is *one* who scatters, yet increases more; / And there is *one* who withholds more than is right, / But it *leads* to poverty." This passage encourages generosity. But it also poses a dilemma: How do we make decisions about sharing our wealth, even as we balance our budgets and save for emergencies?

Five thoughts have helped me to balance my sharing and my saving. I prayerfully consider them whenever I am asked to give, either to a person or to a cause. First, I recognize my wealth is a gift from God. I resist the temptation to think I have gained it by hard work, innate intelligence, or personal magnetism. Deuteronomy 8:17–18 states, "then you say in your heart, 'My power and the might of my hand have gained me this wealth.' And you shall remember the LORD your God, for *it is* He who gives you power to get wealth."

Second, when I give in the right spirit, without compulsion or coercion, my heart enlarges. Saint Paul emphasizes in his Second Epistle to the Corinthians, "*So let* each one *give* as he purposes in his heart, not grudgingly or of necessity; for God loves a cheerful giver" (9:7). Giving out of fear or guilt will not benefit me.

Third, I remember God has provided for my needs in the past. So I try to trust my present and future to Him as well (see Luke 12:6–7).

Fourth, I grow rich in pleasure when I give of *myself*. Either beginning or strengthening a relationship with someone is far more difficult—but far more rewarding—for me than giving away wealth.

Fifth, Jesus Himself said, "It is more blessed to give than to receive" (Acts 20:35). If my giving is sincere, I will indeed experience the joy of the Holy Spirit in my heart.

Font of Wisdom

The saints of the Orthodox Church often speak about "placing the mind in the heart" during prayer. In his first sermon on prayer, titled "A Personal Rule of Prayer," St. Theophan the Recluse (1815–94) clearly explains this phenomenon. He advises:

> Simply enter into every word and then bring the meaning of each word down into your heart. That is, understand what you say, and then experience what you have understood. . . . These two, understanding and feeling—if they are properly carried out—ornament every offering of prayer to the highest quality and make it fruitful and effective.

Before beginning to pray, St. Theophan suggests standing in reverence before the presence of God, establishing a calm inner state, and making a few prostrations before an icon. He also suggests initially reciting a few customary prayers of the Church "without haste," thereby bringing "the meaning of each word down into your heart." If we follow this method, he concludes, "No further rules are necessary."

REFLECTION: *Let me patiently wait for my head to comprehend the words I pray, and then let me convey their meaning to my heart, where I can emotionally experience their depth.*

Hymn from Vespers

As we pass the middle of Lent, by the might of the Cross, let us glorify the mighty God who was lifted up in the midst of the earth. Enable us to behold Your sufferings and Your precious Resurrection, granting us purification and great mercy.

Martyr Matrona of Thessalonica

Matrona of Thessalonica lived during the late third to early fourth century. She knew firsthand the horrors of slavery. As a homeless orphan, she had been auctioned off at a slave block and bought by a wealthy Jewess, Pautila. Thus Matrona became a maid in an affluent and comfortable household.

Matrona's duties included making trips to the market and escorting Pautila to services at the synagogue. While waiting for her mistress to finish worshipping at the synagogue, Matrona often secretly attended Christian services at a nearby hidden church.

On one occasion Matrona stayed longer than usual in the church. Her impatient owner reported her missing slave to the authorities and returned home. When an official went to Pautila's house to gather detailed information about the missing slave, a frightened Matrona came running in, unaware of his presence. During interrogation, Matrona held her tongue about the location of the church and the names of her Christian friends. But she did reveal herself as a Christian, which marked her for martyrdom.

There are two accounts of her martyrdom. One account claims Matrona was beaten mercilessly by her owner, locked in a closet on two occasions, and eventually thrown from the rooftop of her mistress's house. Another account states she was imprisoned and tortured for ministering to fellow Christians and was martyred in 307.

PRAYER: *Blessed Matrona was a simple, dutiful young woman. Help me to be dutiful to You, for You are the Lord and Master of my life.*

TUESDAY   Fourth Week of Great Lent

SCRIPTURE READING: GENESIS 9:8–17

Meditation

The Old Testament records vital covenants between God and His people. Covenants—like treaties—bind parties together. They are also *transactional*: God makes promises to His people, and He demands fidelity of them in return.

We read today of God's covenant with Noah: a rainbow in the sky, signifying God's promise never again to destroy all living creatures by floodwaters (Gen. 9:11). Another famous covenant is God's giving of the Ten Commandments to Moses (Exodus 20). In both instances, God expects His people to strive for holiness in response to His promise. He calls them to claim Him as their only God and, eventually, to become a holy nation.

The New Testament records the "New Covenant" Jesus makes with His disciples at the Last Supper. Jesus had already promised, "He who eats My flesh and drinks My blood abides in Me, and I in him" (John 6:56). And He tells them how to reciprocate: "All that the Father gives Me will come to Me, and the one who comes to Me I will by no means cast out. And this is the will of Him who sent Me, that everyone who sees the Son and believes in Him may have everlasting life; and I will raise him up at the last day" (John 6:37, 40).

Often, I fail miserably as a partner in Jesus' covenant. Yet Jesus Christ my Lord—always faithful—continues to invite me to commune with Him through His Body and Blood, to partake of His New Covenant. As for my part, let me come to Him; let me firmly believe in Him.

Font of Wisdom

In his larger work titled *The Discourses*, St. Symeon the New Theologian (949–1022) includes a chapter titled "God Increases Virtue." Here he relates a predicament of every human being—how to effectively manage one's temper:

> *Again, to be in control of one's temper and anger belongs to a wondrous struggle and extreme effort, but to attain to their complete quiescence and obtain serenity of heart and perfect gentleness is the act of God alone and a transformation at His hand.*

In this passage, St. Symeon succinctly describes the *synergy* between God and human beings. He goes on to explain that in following God's commandments, Christians surely can "sow the seeds of virtue," but "by God's gift and mercy alone the rain of His loving-kindness and grace falls and causes the unfruitful soil of our hearts to bear fruit." In other words, accomplishing any worthwhile deed or obtaining any virtue requires working hand-in-hand with God.

REFLECTION: *On this path to Pascha, let me do my part and allow God to do His part as I struggle with my temper, my anger, and my intolerance.*

Hymn from Vespers

We have completed the third week of the fast. Enable us, O Christ, to behold the wood of Your Cross, to bow before it worthily to attain in purity the holy Resurrection.

Venerable Anthony of the Kiev Far Caves

Anthony was born in 983 in what is now Ukraine. From his youth, he yearned for the ascetic life. He journeyed to Mount Athos and eventually received monastic tonsure. However, his *igumen* (elder or abbot) foresaw the potential of the holy youth as an instructor of other monks, and he sent Anthony back home with his blessing to become an example to others.

Upon returning to Kiev, Anthony settled in a cave hollowed out in the hills above the Dnieper River, where he devoted himself to prayer, fasting, and physical labor. Living a strict life as a hermit, he ate bread and water every other day and often fasted for a full week. Other men soon joined him, among them the monks Nikon and Theodosius. When the community grew to one hundred monks, Anthony appointed Theodosius to be the abbot of the Monastery of the Caves.

The last forty years of Anthony's life were spent in solitary prayer and contemplation in his cave. Still, he counseled many people who were drawn to his holiness. Clearly the Holy Spirit dwelt within him, for he had the gift of clairvoyance and wonderworking. The cave became his tomb when he died in 1073.

Anthony had given spiritual birth to monasticism in his native land. Although he himself had struggled mostly as a solitary hermit, he—understanding the rigors of such an undertaking—also promoted cenobitic, or communal, monastic life as an alternative. About fifty bishops of the Russian Orthodox Church had emerged from his monastery by the year 1250.

PRAYER: *Lord, teach me how to claim time for prayer and solitude with You.*

WEDNESDAY
Fourth Week of Great Lent
SCRIPTURE READING: PROVERBS 12:23—13:9

Meditation

Verse 25 of Proverbs 12 states, "Anxiety in the heart of man causes depression." I know this to be true. An endless number of things worry me, and I become sad over them.

Like weeds choking out beautiful flowers, my cares consume my thoughts and sap my energy, leaving little room for God's peace. In the Gospels (Matt. 6:25–34; Luke 12:22–31), Jesus warns against worry. He assures me His Father in heaven will take care of my needs, if I will "seek first the kingdom of God and His righteousness" (Matt. 6:33).

Similarly, in his Letter to the Philippians St. Paul counsels, "Be anxious for nothing, but in everything by prayer and supplication, with thanksgiving, let your requests be made known to God" (4:6). As I read and reread and absorb those words, I begin to build my trust in God.

God may not remove all small annoyances—or even large obstacles—that trouble me. But He does offer me a different perspective. Through the words of Scripture, I can begin to believe that God is watching over me. He is listening to my requests. He understands my needs. He holds my life in His hands, and He will help me through anxious times.

Font of Wisdom

Christians sometimes believe God requires them to suppress their emotions in a stoic manner. However, St. John Climacus (579–649), a monk at the Monastery of Mount Sinai, declares *all* human emotions are God-created and valuable—if used in the proper manner. In his work *The Ladder of Divine Ascent*—a handbook outlining successive steps to obtaining Christian virtues—in Step 26, titled "On Discernment," St. John writes:

> *God neither caused nor created evil and, therefore, those who assert that certain passions come naturally to the soul are quite wrong. What they fail to realize is that we have taken natural attributes of our own and turned them into passions.*

Saint John gives several examples. He differentiates between sexual desire within the bonds of marriage (including the procreation of children) and fornication. He urges that anger, arrogance, and resentment be directed against Satan instead of our neighbor. He suggests directing the natural wish to compete toward outdoing one another in developing virtue. He recognizes the human need for food but eschews gluttony.

REFLECTION: *Have I been trying to suppress my emotional life rather than directing my natural emotions toward good ends, leading to an abundant inner life (John 10:10)?*

Hymn from Presanctified Liturgy

The fast now has brought us midway through its course. Having pleased God with the days that have passed, we look forward to making good use of the days to come, for growth in blessings brings forth even greater achievements. While pleasing Christ, we cry: O Lord, make us worthy to share in Your Paschal victory.

Hieromartyr Mark, Bishop of Arethusa

Mark lived in the early fourth century, during the time Emperor Constantine had stopped the persecution of Christians. As an enthusiastic young priest, Mark was responsible for destroying a pagan temple and replacing it with a Christian church—an act encouraged by the state. During Constantine's reign, a religious transformation occurred in society. Crosses replaced pagan idols. Pagan temples were dismantled piece by piece and either rebuilt as Christian churches or converted into hospitals and houses of refuge for the poor and needy.

Eventually, Mark was consecrated bishop of Arethusa, in the province of Thessalonica. He won many converts to Christ because of his genuine concern and compassion for people and because of his humility and deep faith.

Mark pursued his mission to destroy vestiges of paganism until Julian the Apostate became emperor in 361. Then Christians once again underwent persecution. Mark endured unbelievable tortures after he refused to repay his pagan tormentors money to rebuild the temple he had destroyed. His persecutors slashed his body, pulled out his hair, dragged him through the mud, and even cut off his ears. They smeared his body with honey and hung him in a basket to be bitten by wasps, bees, and hornets.

After being astounded by Mark's courage, as well as his continued refusal to pay them any money, his adversaries released him. Mark continued to preach, and he converted many to the Faith. He died in 389.

PRAYER: *Each time I enter Your church, Lord, let me remember that it is a holy and sanctified place.*

THURSDAY   Fourth Week of Great Lent

SCRIPTURE READING: GENESIS 10:32—11:9

Meditation

Today's story about the Tower of Babel begins with people building a great city to glorify their own ability and to make a great name for themselves. They had discovered unity and purpose without the One True God, and so their potential to sin was unlimited. Biblical historians tell us the great tower of their new city was intended to reach the heavens and the gods they worshipped.

This story jars me. I'm reminded of my Lord's words, "for without Me you can do nothing" (John 15:5). Yet I often take pride in my accomplishments. I recognize the value of hard work, study, preparation, practice, and diligence. I like to think I can accomplish things by myself, due to my own effort and ability. My ways are so much like the ways of the people in this story. I even think I can reach spiritual maturity on my own.

I forget God alone grants me my ability, strength, and talent to bring projects to their full potential. I sin by ignoring the time-honored Orthodox practice of beginning any activity with prayer and ending it with thanksgiving.

God does not want me to divorce my daily activities from Him. Let me begin to see Him as the source of all things. Let me base my worth on His value of me and not on my own accomplishments.

Font of Wisdom

Saint Gregory of Sinai (circa 1260–1346), a monk of Mount Athos, was instrumental in the development of *hesychasm*, or union with God through "stillness of the heart." Under experienced spiritual guides, hesychasts learned to repeat "Lord, Jesus Christ, Son of God, be merciful to me, a sinner" until the prayer reverberated in their hearts continuously.

Saint Gregory's essay "On Divine Energy," found in *The Philokalia*—a collection of texts by spiritual masters—describes the effects of grace on the heart:

> *The energy of grace is the power of spiritual fire that fills the heart with joy and gladness, stabilizes, warms and purifies the soul, temporarily stills our provocative thoughts, and for a time suspends the body's impulsions. The signs and fruits that testify to its authenticity are tears, contrition, humility, self-control, silence, patience, self-effacement and similar qualities, all of which constitute undeniable evidence of its presence.*

REFLECTION: *Let my aim in prayer be having the Holy Spirit indwell my heart, rather than having God ease my daily drudgery by answering all my requests.*

Hymn from Vespers

Your martyrs, O Lord, did not forsake You. Nor did they turn from Your commandments. By their prayers, have mercy on us.

Venerable John Climacus of Sinai
COMMEMORATED MARCH 30/APRIL 12
& FOURTH SUNDAY OF GREAT LENT

Little is known about the life of St. John of the Ladder, also known as St. John Climacus. According to some sources, he was born in 579. He was tonsured a monk, then spent forty years in solitude before becoming abbot of St. Catherine's Monastery on Mount Sinai. After serving four years as head of that monastery, he is said to have reposed at age seventy-five.

The Greek word *klimakos* means "ladder." The name was given to John because he wrote a popular book titled *The Ladder of Divine Ascent*. The book was originally intended as a guide for monks, but it has proven valuable for all Christians. The title "The Ladder" was inspired by the biblical story of the Old Testament Patriarch Jacob, who in a vision saw a ladder extending from earth to heaven (see Gen. 28:12).

The book is divided into thirty chapters, or "steps," which describe an ascetic journey from sinfulness to spiritual perfection. The first seven steps pertain to virtues necessary for the ascetic life. Steps 8–26 give instruction on overcoming vices and strengthening their corresponding virtues. The final four steps relate to the higher virtues toward which the ascetic life aims. The final step on the ladder is love.

PRAYER: *I get discouraged when I slide backward on the journey to Your Kingdom, Lord. Help me to persevere without despair.*

Fourth Week of Great Lent
SCRIPTURE READING: ISAIAH 29:13–23

Meditation

Many aspects of Orthodox liturgical life, with its structure and ritual, are the very things that so easily lead us away from true worship. In today's reading from Isaiah, God expresses His displeasure with those who claim to be His even though their hearts are far away. He does not desire worship by rote.

The words of church prayers and the liturgy are so familiar to me that I breeze through them without contemplation. With little feeling and little thought, I hurriedly repeat prayers without stilling my heart in order to hear what God is saying to me.

I treat the sacraments carelessly. I approach Holy Confession by measuring myself against my neighbor (thereby seeing myself favorably), instead of viewing myself against the stature of Christ. I habitually come week after week to Holy Communion without preparation, failing to recognize the consuming fire to which I draw near.

I am equally careless about holy things. When I hear admonishments about proper church behavior, I say to myself, "This doesn't apply to me—perhaps to the person on the other side of the church—but not to me."

God desires me to worship Him with an attentive and willing heart. I see myself, however, casually going through the motions of my Faith. Let me allow God's Spirit to touch and guide my life of worship.

Font of Wisdom

Saint Innocent of Alaska (1797–1879), renowned missionary to North America and Metropolitan of Moscow in his later years, writes remarkably about humility in his work *Indication of the Way* to the *Kingdom of Heaven.* He insists that action by the Holy Spirit is essential to understanding our true spiritual condition, including our motivations and virtues.

"The Holy Spirit gives true humility," he says simply. "Even the most intelligent person, if he has not the Holy Spirit, cannot know himself properly." He goes on:

> But when the Holy Spirit dwells in the heart of a person, He shows him all his inner poverty and weakness, and the corruption of his heart and soul, and his separation from God; and with all his virtues and righteousness, He shows him his sin, his sloth and indifference regarding the salvation and good of people, his self-seeking in his apparently most disinterested virtues, his coarse selfishness even where he does not suspect it. The Holy Spirit shows him everything as it really is.

REFLECTION: *On my spiritual journey, am I becoming humble enough to admit I owe whatever virtue I possess solely to God?*

Hymn from Vespers

My soul's nobility has been enslaved to passions. Like a beast, I cannot lift up my eyes to You, O Most High. But bowing down, I pray like the publican and cry: Have mercy on me, O God, and save me.

Innocent, Metropolitan of Moscow, Enlightener of the Aleuts, Apostle to America

COMMEMORATED MARCH 31/APRIL 13 (REPOSE)
& SEPTEMBER 23/OCTOBER 6 (CANONIZATION)

John Popov was born August 27, 1797, in Anginsk, a small village near Irkutsk, Siberia. At age six, he was already reading during church services. At age nine, he entered the Irkutsk seminary, where he remained for eleven years. Besides his seminary classes, he studied history and the sciences, and he learned carpentry, furniture making, blacksmithing, and the construction of musical instruments. John married and was ordained to the priesthood in 1821.

Against the wishes of family and friends, the priest John volunteered to preach in Unalaska, in the Aleutian Islands. He and his family reached their post after a rigorous fourteen-month journey. He taught the natives carpentry and furniture making—skills they used to construct a home, chapel, and the Cathedral of the Holy Ascension.

His primary work was educating the natives in the Orthodox Faith and drawing them into the Church. He learned their languages and culture. He translated church services and the Gospel of Matthew into their native tongue. He also wrote a book in Aleut: *The Indication of the Way into the Kingdom of Heaven*, which eventually appeared in more than forty editions. His work in geography, ethnography, and linguistics received worldwide acclaim.

In 1834 Father John was transferred to Sitka. After his wife died, he became a monk, and in 1840 he was consecrated bishop of Kamchatka, the Kurile and Aleutian Islands; he was later raised to the rank of archbishop. In 1868 he succeeded Metropolitan Philaret on the Moscow cathedra. He died on Holy Saturday in 1879.

PRAYER: *Saint Innocent served You with all his varied talents, Lord. May I serve You with the talents You have given me.*

SATURDAY   Fourth Week of Great Lent

Meditation

When I was a child, I took great comfort in the wonderful stories of Jesus healing people; the blind, the deaf, and the lame went on their ways with health restored. In my child's mind I was convinced if some physical tragedy befell me, Jesus would heal me, and I would be made whole again.

Believing is much more difficult for me now. Jesus promises He will hear my prayer and answer it. Yet, I see people all around me who are terribly afflicted. The deaf, blind, and paralyzed, and those with cancer and an assortment of other maladies, are *not* all healed.

When I witness this confounding situation, I must remember: I was also taught as a child to ask Jesus to do *His* will, not mine. As I grow closer to my Lord, I realize His answers to my prayers may not be in the form I want—or expect. I may not be healed physically if my bodily ailments are necessary for me to be healed of some spiritual sickness. The kind of miracle I expect may not be as advantageous as the solution God is providing for my ultimate spiritual healing.

Many times, only when I look back on difficulties do I recognize that God was with me. He answered my prayers. His answer was best for me, for His response brought me closer to Him. Just as in today's Gospel reading Jesus healed a man from physical deafness, He can heal my spiritual deafness. I take great comfort in this.

Font of Wisdom

In his spiritual counsel preserved in *The Little Russian Philokalia*, St. Seraphim of Sarov (1754–1833) speaks of the importance of uninterrupted prayer. He advises, for example, to keep one's eyes closed during the church services "in internal mindfulness," and he warns "not to give oneself up to dispersion of thoughts." He also tells readers to practice prayer as often as possible:

Those who have truly decided to serve the Lord God should practice the remembrance of God and uninterrupted prayer to Jesus Christ, mentally saying: Lord Jesus Christ, Son of God, have mercy on me a sinner. . . . By such exercises in preserving oneself from dispersion and keeping peace of conscience one may draw near to God and be united to Him. For in the words of St. Isaac the Syrian: "Without uninterrupted prayer we cannot draw near to God."

REFLECTION: *Let me disrupt my daily routine—already full of interruptions—by saying on occasion, "Lord Jesus Christ, Son of God, be merciful to me, a sinner."*

Hymn from Vespers

Let us honor John Climacus, that pride of ascetics, that angel on earth, that man of God in heaven, that adornment of the world, and that example of virtue and good deeds. For, planted in the house of God, he flourished with justice; and like a cedar in the wilderness, he caused the flock of Christ to grow.

Venerable Seraphim, Wonderworker of Sarov

COMMEMORATED JANUARY 2/15 (REPOSE)
& JULY 19/AUGUST 1 (UNCOVERING OF RELICS)

Seraphim, a well-known and beloved saint of the Russian Orthodox Church, was born in 1754 in Kursk. His parents, Isidore and Agathia Moshnin, named him Prochorus. After the death of his father, he was raised piously by his widowed mother.

Once he learned to read, Prochorus immersed himself in Christian literature: Holy Scripture, especially the Psalms, and the lives of the saints. He spent all the time he could in church services, and at age nineteen, he decided to dedicate himself to God by pursuing a monastic vocation. After years of obedience, he was tonsured a monk at age twenty-seven and received the name Seraphim, which was indicative of the flame of love for the Lord in his heart. Eventually, Seraphim was ordained a deacon and then a priest.

Seraphim's life, from childhood on, was characterized by intense prayer and solitude. For many years he lived as a hermit in the forest near his monastery. For one thousand days and nights he spent the better part of his time kneeling on a stone and constantly praying, "O God, be merciful to me, a sinner." The wild animals were his sole company, except when he returned to his monastery church to receive Holy Communion.

His life was also marked by miracles and especially by significant visitations from the Mother of God, who acted as his healer on many occasions. During one Divine Liturgy Seraphim even saw a vision of Jesus Christ, causing him to stand immobile in ecstasy for several hours.

During the last years of his life, the Mother of God appeared to Seraphim and instructed him to open his cell door to others and to become a spiritual guide. His counsel was sought by thousands. His most famous encounter is recorded in a document titled, "Conversation of Saint Seraphim of Sarov with N.A. Motovilov." In this conversation, Seraphim explains that the goal of the Christian life is to acquire the peace of the Holy Spirit within.

Seraphim addressed everyone as "my joy." He greeted all who came to see him with a prostration, a kiss, and the Paschal greeting, "Christ is risen!" He died in 1833.

PRAYER: *By loving You foremost, St. Seraphim found joy in each person he encountered. Teach me to do the same, Lord.*

SUNDAY
Fourth Week of Great Lent
Sunday of Saint John Climacus
SCRIPTURE READING: MARK 9:17–31

Meditation

Today's reading describes the healing of a boy who had a "mute spirit." After Jesus' disciples fail to heal the boy, the child's father asks the Lord Himself for help. The father cries out tearfully, "Lord, I believe; help my unbelief!" (Mark 9:24). Accepting both his sincere faith and his humble admission, Jesus heals his son. Later, the disciples privately ask Jesus why they had been not been able to cast out the spirit. Jesus tells them that nothing but prayer and fasting works in such cases. Why?

If the disciples had prayed and fasted, they would have realized they could not accomplish anything without the help of God. They would have understood they were not the source of the healing power that had been given to them—Jesus was (see Matt. 10:1). They would have arrived at the same humble state of mind as the boy's father, who professed total dependence on Jesus.

Through prayer and fasting, I realize the weakness of my own soul and body, which are so feeble. I begin to understand the frailty of my being and my absolute reliance on God. I start to comprehend the shallowness of my belief and the depth of my unbelief. Prayer and fasting help me to have the kind of humble faith that will make all things "possible to him who believes" (Mark 9:23).

Font of Wisdom

Saint John Climacus (579–649), a monk of Mount Sinai, writes about simplicity in prayer in Step 28 of his spiritual classic *The Ladder of Divine Ascent*. He reminds fellow Christians:

> *In your prayers there is no need for high-flown words, for it is the simple and unsophisticated babblings of children that have more often won the heart of the Father in Heaven. Try not to talk excessively in your prayer, in case your mind is distracted by the search for words. One word from the publican sufficed to placate God, and a single utterance saved the thief.*

He also advises beginning times of prayer with the humble words, "Have mercy on me, for I am weak."

REFLECTION: *Let me humbly commit to keeping my prayers simple.*

Hymn from Divine Liturgy

O dweller of the wilderness and angel in the body, you were a wonder-worker, O Father John Climacus. You received heavenly gifts through fasting, vigil, and prayer, healing the sick and the souls of those drawn to you by faith. Glory to Him who gave you strength.

Andrew, Archbishop of Crete

COMMEMORATED JULY 4/17

Andrew was born in Damascus in the seventh century. Up until age seven, he was mute and did not speak. He was healed of this impediment by receiving the Holy Eucharist. From that day on he earnestly studied the Holy Scripture and the theology of the Church.

As an adolescent, Andrew entered the St. Sava the Sanctified

Monastery near Jerusalem, accepting monastic tonsure. He was regarded as meek and chaste, and he possessed a superb intellect. In 680 Patriarch Theodore of Jerusalem selected him as a representative to the Sixth Ecumenical Council in Constantinople. There the now archdeacon Andrew demonstrated his skill as a theologian when he argued against the Monothelite heresy, which erroneously taught that Jesus Christ had only one will (divine) instead of two natural wills, human and divine.

Andrew remained in the city, where he served in the Great Church of Constantinople and was assigned to be in charge of an orphanage and a hospice for old men. Eventually, he was elevated to the episcopacy and made bishop of Gortineia, the metropolitan see of the island of Crete.

For the rest of his life, Andrew distinguished himself as a preacher and hymnographer, leaving a permanent mark on the Byzantine Liturgy. He introduced the form of hymnody now known as a "canon." He is remembered most specifically for his Great Penitential Canon, which is still used during Great Lent. The year of his repose is uncertain: 726 or even 740.

PRAYER: *As I approach You this Lenten season, Lord, let my repentance be sincere, and forgive my sins.*

MONDAY   Fifth Week of Great Lent

SCRIPTURE READING: GENESIS 13:12–18

Meditation

Today's Scripture teaches us about the importance of choices. Abram leaves his home with his family and departs for the land of Canaan, as the Lord commands. However, because of strife between the herdsmen of Abram's livestock and the herdsmen of his nephew Lot's livestock, Abram generously and peaceably gives Lot his choice of land—allowing room for both wealthy families to settle comfortably in their new surroundings.

Lot picks a spot among the cities of the valley and moves his tent as far as the city of Sodom. He freely chooses land full of great possessions and compromising enticements common to civilization. But Abram elects an area where God is the only enticement. He desires only the Lord to live in the midst of him and his family.

Their choices are significant. Each man is called, but only Abram, because of his faithfulness, is chosen to inherit the Promised Land. He chooses to be with the Lord rather than in the land of wickedness. He accepts the Lord's invitation to serve Him forever.

I too am called to dwell in the presence of God and to serve Him alone. "For many are called, but few chosen," I read in Matthew 20:16. At times, I wish *all* were called and *all* were chosen. But God's call and His gift of free will require my response. I can choose to be with the Lord, or I can separate myself from Him.

Font of Wisdom

Saint Isaac the Syrian, in his seventh-century work *Ascetical Homilies*, presents an exquisite vision of communion with God. His words recall Jesus' own: "I am the bread of life" (John 6:35).

> *The man who has found love eats and drinks Christ every day and hour and thereby is made immortal. "He that eateth of this bread," He says, "which I will give him, shall not see death unto eternity." Blessed is he who consumes the bread of love, which is Jesus!*

Saint Isaac explains that love comprises the heavenly banquet in the Kingdom of God. He rhetorically asks, "For when we hear Him say, 'Ye shall eat and drink at the table of My Kingdom,' what do we suppose we shall eat, if not love?" He concludes that every human being "who lives in love reaps the fruit of life from God" and "breathes the air of the resurrection"—even while still on earth.

REFLECTION: *Do I often consider the true aim of my Lenten pilgrimage—love?*

Hymn from Vespers

Like the blind man, I cry from my heart: Enlighten the eyes of my heart, O Son of God. . . . My soul is possessed by pleasure's demons. When You deliver it from the darkness of passions, enable me to spend the rest of my life in purity that I might glorify Your great goodness.

Venerable Anthony the Great
COMMEMORATED JANUARY 17/30

Anthony, born in upper Egypt in 251, inherited a wealthy estate from his parents. Soon after their deaths, Anthony heard the Holy Gospel reading in which Christ tells the rich young man, "If you want to be perfect, go, sell what you have and give to the poor, and you will have treasure in heaven; and come, follow Me" (Matt. 19:21). The passage inspired Anthony to sell his estate and give the proceeds to the poor.

Anthony first moved into a modest hut, earning a living by his own hands and giving the proceeds to the poor; then he moved out of the city into a graveyard tomb; and finally he settled in the desert to live a life totally dedicated to God. With each successive move, Anthony struggled more vigorously with prayer, fasting, and solitude. And with each successive move, assaults on him from demonic forces grew fiercer.

Demons came to him through obscene imaginings. They also came in physical forms, savagely beating him. Anthony opposed these assaults by strict watchfulness over his senses, austere fasting, and prayer—and especially by wielding the Life-giving Cross against the demons.

When the initial assaults ended, Anthony cried out to God, "Where have You been, O merciful Jesus? Why didn't You appear from the very beginning to end my pain?"

Jesus replied, "I was here, Anthony, but I wanted to see your struggle. Now, since you have not yielded, I shall always help you and make your name known throughout all the world."

In all Anthony spent eighty-five years in the desert. Because of his profound wisdom and counsel, great crowds often attempted to visit him, disrupting his solitude. Even Emperor Constantine and his sons sought Anthony's advice. However, Anthony came out of the desert only during dire circumstances: either to defend Orthodox doctrine against heretical uprisings, or to accompany martyrs to their places of execution, comforting them and volunteering to die with them, if the Lord willed. Anthony reposed at age 105, peacefully, in his desert dwelling.

PRAYER: *Lord Jesus Christ, grant me patience and fortitude, both in everyday struggles and in my lifelong journey toward Your Kingdom.*

TUESDAY   Fifth Week of Great Lent

SCRIPTURE READING: PROVERBS 15:7–19

Meditation

Of all God's creatures, human beings alone have the gift of speech. Although it is an ultimate gift, speech also can pose an ultimate danger. Words can heal, but they can also kill; words can inspire, but they can also poison.

Today's reading reminds me to guard against idle talk:

The lips of the wise disperse knowledge
But the heart of the fool does not do so. . . .
The heart of him who has understanding seeks knowledge
But the mouth of fools feeds on foolishness. (Prov. 15:7, 14)

I may ponder: How often do my unguarded words feed on folly? Do I spread idle rumors about others? Do I gossip? Are my words directed by, and to, God?

My words can be prideful or humble, judgmental or forgiving. They can be either like the words of the Pharisee or like the words of the publican (see Luke 18:9–14). Ultimately, I will be responsible to God for all words I have uttered. Jesus Christ warned, "But I say to you that for every idle word men may speak, they will give account of it in the day of judgment. For by your words you will be justified, and by your words you will be condemned" (Matt. 12:36–37).

The Lenten prayer of St. Ephraim the Syrian instructs me in protecting the sanctity, holiness, and power of words. I ask the Lord and Master of my life to take from me the spirit of "idle talk."

Font of Wisdom

Saint Tikhon of Zadonsk (1724–83) compares reading the Holy Bible to reading a letter from God Himself. He writes:

> *The King of Heaven has sent a letter to you, an earthly and mortal man.... Whenever you read the gospel, Christ Himself is speaking to you. And while you read, you are praying and talking with Him. God speaks to man; the King of Heaven talks with the corruptible creature; the Lord holds conversation with the servant.*

Saint Tikhon finds it incredible that human beings gladly read correspondence from a person of importance—such as an earthly ruler—but neglect to read the Holy Bible. He himself looks upon Scripture as a merciful gift that reveals God's will and offers God's guidance on how to live. "What can be more pleasant ... more instructive?" he inquires.

REFLECTION: *Let me begin to look upon Holy Scripture as God's letter filled with His mercy and love—a letter personally addressed to me.*

Hymn from Vespers

Let us control our passions through abstinence. Let us have love as our food. Let us strive to live acceptably for God, who accepted the Cross and the spear. In this way we shall enjoy the food of eternal life.

Venerable Zosimas, Monk of Palestine
COMMEMORATED APRIL 4/17

Zosimas was born in the fifth century, during the reign of Emperor Theodosius the Younger. By his own account, he entered a monastery in Palestine after he was weaned from his mother. He resided within the monastery's walls for fifty-three years and became a *hieromonk* (priest-monk), having earned everyone's respect for his ascetic life and wise counsel. Zosimas had a single aim: to sing praises to God and to practice the teachings of the Holy Scriptures.

As the years passed, however, Zosimas became obsessed by one thought: He himself was perfect, and he needed no instruction from anyone. He said to himself, "Is there a man to be found in the desert who has surpassed me in holiness?" In answer to his question, an angel appeared and instructed him to move to a stricter monastery by the Jordan River. His renowned ascetic labors and resultant wisdom attracted monks from neighboring monasteries.

During one of the monks' annual forty-day Lenten retreats into the desert across the Jordan, Zosimas discovered Mary of Egypt. Once having lived as a prostitute, this woman had repented and had lived as a hermit in the desert for decades, fighting her former passions. She had far surpassed Zosimas in ascetical effort and holiness. Zosimas's encounter with the saintly Mary changed his life, for her story of true repentance brought him the virtue of humility.

PRAYER: *Lord, take from me any pride that separates me from others.*

WEDNESDAY   Fifth Week of Great Lent

SCRIPTURE READING: ISAIAH 41:4–14

Meditation

In the Book of the Prophet Isaiah, the prophet receives a dire message from God: The Kingdom of Judah will be saved from invasion by the Assyrians, but the Babylonian army will capture it instead, and its people will be exiled because of their disobedience to the Lord. Later, Babylon itself will be overthrown, and God will return the exiles to their homeland.

Despite what lay ahead for Judah, today's reading keeps emphasizing God's comforting words: "Fear not, for I *am* with you; / Be not dismayed, for I *am* your God. / I will strengthen you, / Yes, I will help you, / I will uphold you with My righteous right hand" (41:10). Through the prophet's words, God calms and encourages the Hebrew nation—even in the face of impending persecution. Despite their disobedience, the Lord will always protect and preserve His people from their enemies.

Just as the words of the prophet comforted the people of the Old Testament, New Testament Scripture encourages followers of Jesus. Saint Paul writes, "Watch, stand fast in the faith, be brave, be strong" (1 Cor. 16:13). Jesus Himself told His disciples, "In the world you will have tribulation; but be of good cheer, I have overcome the world" (John 16:33).

Fear often clouds my judgment and leaves me confused. When I'm afraid to press on, let me call upon the name of the Lord, for He is my protector, my helper.

Font of Wisdom

In his work *My Life in Christ*, St. John of Kronstadt (1829–1909) says a lot about trusting God as a "most merciful, all-powerful, most wise, everloving, ever-perfect" Father—come what may. "Trust in him," says St. John, "in respect of the blessings of this temporal life, but above all, in respect of the future blessings which shall be granted you in Christ Jesus." With trust in God, he affirms, one can be calm in every circumstance, rich though impoverished, and assured of forgiveness, no matter the sin. He writes:

> *The Lord is everything to you, and you must be everything to the Lord. As all your treasure is in your heart and your will, and God asks of you your heart, saying, "My son, give me thine heart," therefore in order to fulfill God's perfect will, renounce your own corrupt, wayward, plausible will, and know it not; know only God's will. Not my will, but thine be done.*

REFLECTION: *Usually, what I really want when I pray is simply God's "stamp of approval" on my own plans. Let me try to sincerely pray "Your will be done."*

Hymn from the Canon of St. Andrew of Crete

Wild beasts surround me, but snatch me from them, O Savior. For You desire all to be saved and to come to the knowledge of the truth. As their Creator, save them and with them, save me. Save me before I completely perish, O Lord.

Venerable Alexis, the Man of God

Born and educated in Rome in the fifth century, Alexis was the only son of a rich senator. Based on the example of his charitable parents, he likened alms given to the poor to eternal treasures transferred to heaven.

Alexis fled his privileged life and ended up in the city of Edessa, where he lived under a portico near a church dedicated to the Mother of God. He embraced utter poverty, and eventually his appearance drastically changed as his body withered away from fasting. He lived this way for seventeen years until an icon of the Theotokos within the church revealed his holiness. A voice spoke from the icon, calling Alexis "the man of God."

In deep humility and fearing earthly praise, Alexis returned to Rome incognito and begged his own father to allow him to live in a corner of his courtyard. Alexis's father did not recognize him, but he received his beloved child as a common beggar and cared for his needs. For seventeen more years Alexis lived unrecognized on his father's property, bearing in patience and silence the ill-treatment of the household servants. He also suffered emotional distress in witnessing the mourning of his parents—and the young wife he had abandoned—for their "lost" son and husband.

Only at Alexis's death was his identity revealed. He had written down his name and an account of his life and clasped the message in his hand as he reposed. The emperor and pope carried the body of Alexis into the Church of St. Peter, where it remained one week before being placed in a marble crypt. The relics of the saint, which gushed fragrant myrrh, eventually were buried in the Church of St. Boniface and were uncovered in 1216.

PRAYER: *Lord, St. Alexis accepted humiliation at great personal cost. Let me learn from his life when I need to be humbled.*

Meditation

In Orthodox Tradition pride is often identified as the root of all sin and humility as the mother of all virtue. Today's Scripture likewise teaches me, "Pride *goes* before destruction, / And a haughty spirit before a fall" (16:18).

Do I really believe this? Don't I usually see humility as weakness and pride as strength? And don't I even *encourage* myself to believe that way? After all, my surrounding culture teaches me to fight for my rights, to be assertive (even selfish), and to be somewhat obnoxiously proud of my achievements.

Jesus Christ teaches the contrary: "For whoever exalts himself will be humbled, and he who humbles himself will be exalted" (Luke 14:11). The liturgical texts during Great Lent—the Canon of St. Andrew of Crete and the prayer of St. Ephraim the Syrian—give me the same message.

If only I would begin to *live* the teachings of my Tradition, and not merely listen to them! Perhaps then I would understand the way of the Lamb of God, who, through His own humility on the Cross, was exalted. Perhaps I could then see how my pride dishonors me and how it diminishes the person God created me to be.

Font of Wisdom

Saint Ignatius Brianchaninov (1807–67), renowned Russian patristics scholar, offers much instruction about the famous prayer, "Lord, Jesus Christ, Son of God, be merciful to me, a sinner." In his work *On the Prayer of Jesus*, he corrects the assumption that prayer is always a time of joyful praise, writing a rather scary thought:

It is of the nature of inner prayer to reveal the hidden passions con-
cealed in the human heart and to tame them. Inner prayer shows
us our captivity to the fallen spirits, making us realize our impris-
onment and freeing us from it.

Saint Ignatius assures readers, however, there is no need for distress when disturbing and perplexing negative thoughts and feelings arise during prayer. Such passions, he claims, can be tamed by persistently, calmly, and unhurriedly reciting the Jesus Prayer—even as a great inner struggle ensues. "This is the time of hidden martyrdom," he writes. But he also promises that devotion to prayer and faithfulness to the Lord "will invariably bring us victory."

REFLECTION: *Let me become brave enough to confront my negative*
thoughts and feelings, armed with the promise of inner freedom through
prayer.

Hymn from Matins

Dressed in the armor of faith, armed with the sign of the Cross, you are
soldiers who were worthy of God. Courageously you opposed the tortur-
ers, crushing the devil's deceits. You were victors, made worthy of crowns.
O martyrs, pray to Christ for us, to save our souls.

John the Merciful, Patriarch of Alexandria
COMMEMORATED NOVEMBER 12/25

John, a wealthy widower whose children had died, became renowned for using his income to help the poor. His continuing generosity and personal holiness led him to be chosen as patriarch of Alexandria around 608, when he was about fifty years old.

When he arrived in Alexandria—the richest, most prestigious city in the East—the new patriarch took under his protection more than seven thousand poor people of the city, whom he considered to be his "masters." He distributed the gold of the church's treasury to hospitals and monasteries. Under his watch, the needy received all contributions that came into the patriarch's office. When his stewards complained he was impoverishing the church, he replied, "God will provide." When the Persians plundered Jerusalem, John helped refugees fleeing to Egypt by sending them food, wine, and money.

John himself lived in austerity. Once, having received a richly woven bed-covering from a benefactor, he sold the item and gave the money to the poor. The donor rebought the item several more times and presented it again and again to John—with the same result. The patriarch is said to have remarked drily, "We will see who tires first."

John also made time to listen to his people and to resolve their problems. His greatest joy was in reconciling brothers and sisters in Christ. On one occasion, aware that members of his congregation often amused themselves outside the church during the Divine Liturgy, John followed them out and sat among them. "The shepherd must be with his flock," he explained. The churchgoers never repeated their irreverence!

PRAYER: *Help me to be generous with my possessions, Lord, for all I claim as mine comes from You.*

Meditation

In today's Scripture, God tests Abraham by commanding him to sacrifice his son, Isaac, as a burnt offering. Abraham responds with complete faithfulness. He obeys his Lord and goes to the mountain to slay his child. But God stops him and provides a ram for Abraham to use in Isaac's place, saying, "for now I know that you fear God, since you have not withheld your son, your only *son*, from Me" (Gen. 22:12).

I have always stood in awe before this story. Here is Abraham, who has been promised to become the father of many nations; he and his wife have prayed for a son for many years. Finally, Isaac is born to them, and now God wants Abraham to kill his only son. How should I interpret this dramatic event?

At the very heart of this story is the issue of faith in God. Abraham believes in God. He trusts Him. He is fully convinced that God can do what He promised. Certainly, Abraham loves Isaac, but he clearly loves God more. The Lord God is his master, and he faithfully obeys Him—even when it's illogical, even when he believes he will lose the son God said would eventually make him "a great nation" (Gen. 12:2).

At times, I wonder how far I would go to obey God. Would I trust God in everything? Would I love Him above all else? Would I believe in His promises to me, even when He seems to direct me on a path diametrically opposed to them? During times of mistrust, let me recall the story of Abraham and Isaac on the mountain.

Font of Wisdom

In his *Homily XI On 1 Timothy*, St. John Chrysostom (347–407), archbishop of Constantinople, uses words commonly paraphrased nowadays as "You can't take it with you." Saint John regards wealth not as personal property, but rather as a loan. He notes that upon death all human beings leave their possessions to others—*ad infinitum*—and so he preaches:

> Our goods here are not our own; we have only a life interest in them, or rather they fail us [even] during our lives. Only virtues of the soul are properly our own, as almsgiving and charity. For we cannot take our wealth with us when we depart from hence, but we can take our charities. . . . But let us rather send them before us, that they may prepare for us an abode in the eternal mansions (Luke 16:9).

Saint John urges his listeners to extinguish their "love of wealth" and to kindle in themselves instead a "desire for eternal things."

REFLECTION: *Am I remembering to give alms during Great Lent, in the form of either comfort or aid to others?*

Hymn from Vespers

Once Adam was deceived: He sought to become God and failed. Now Christ becomes human in order to make Adam god. Glory to You, O God!

John Chrysostom, Archbishop of Constantinople
COMMEMORATED NOVEMBER 13/26

John was born around the year 347 in Antioch, Syria. Even as a youth he was recognized as an eloquent orator. After his education, he joined a loose-knit community of monks and spent two years in solitude in a cave—standing, keeping vigil, and memorizing the Holy Bible.

John was ordained to the priesthood at about age forty. He was given the responsibility of preaching for his aging bishop in Antioch; he preached several days a week, and frequently several times a day. During Great Lent in 387, John delivered a memorable series of sermons titled *On the Statues* in response to a major political and social crisis. Citizens had revolted over an increase in taxes and had pulled down statues of Emperor Theodosius and his family. In twenty-one homilies, John directly dealt with the circumstances and guided his flock, who feared imperial retribution.

After John was consecrated archbishop of Constantinople in 398, he zealously reduced the expenses of the diocese. Funds from savings went to the poor and to hospitals. He also founded monastic communities for women.

John expressed strong views on many moral issues. While inflexible toward the impenitent, he showed great compassion toward the repentant. Partly due to his fiery sermons, containing unyielding messages regarding moral behavior, he incurred the wrath of the imperial court and was ultimately exiled. At one point during his cruel exile his strength failed him during a forced march, and he died in Comana in 407.

The designation of Chrysostom, or "Golden Mouth," was given to John after his death. Besides his numerous homilies on Scripture, he wrote most of the eucharistic prayers of the Divine Liturgy that bears his name. The Church also annually proclaims his famous catechetical sermon on Pascha each year.

PRAYER: *Lord, let only virtuous words come from my mouth.*

SATURDAY   Fifth Week of Great Lent

SCRIPTURE READING: HEBREWS 9:24–28

Meditation

Today's reading explains how Jesus Christ has fulfilled—and forever changed—the worship of the Hebrew nation, as recorded in the Old Testament. Old Testament worship first centered around the tabernacle in the desert and then around the temple in Jerusalem. God's forgiveness was granted and sealed by the blood of sacrificed animals offered by the high priest. The manner of worship for God's chosen people had been dictated by the Lord down to the last detail. All of this was good, but it only pointed to a future reality that would replace the Old Covenant and usher in the New Covenant between God and His new "holy nation" (1 Pet. 2:9).

The Book of Hebrews spells out this monumental shift in worship. Now Christ is the High Priest, and His priesthood is far superior to the priesthood of the Old Covenant. His Body is the tabernacle and the temple. He is the sacrifice and, by His Blood, forgiveness is ours. He has written the law of love on our hearts. Through Him, heaven has been opened, and it far outshines the mere copy of it that was the temple in Jerusalem. By tasting His precious Body and Blood, we can already taste the bliss of His Kingdom.

Let me accept the "New Covenant" that Christ offers me, for I realize my salvation is found in Him alone. May I run to Him openly and joyfully!

Font of Wisdom

In his work *My Life in Christ*, St. John of Kronstadt (1829–1909), renowned pastor and wonderworker of Russia, writes movingly about what it means to follow the biblical command "You shall love your neighbor as yourself" (Mark 12:31). His keen message jolts the conscience:

> We stand before the altar of love, before the very presence of Love Incarnate himself; and we have no love for each other! Is it not strange? And worse, we do not even worry about it, do not care about it. But love will not come of itself—we must strive for it with earnest efforts. . . . Love every man as yourself—that is, do not wish him anything that you do not wish for yourself; think, feel, for him, just as you would think and feel for your own self; do not wish to see in him anything that you do not wish to see in yourself. . . . Do unto them as you would to yourself, and not otherwise, and you will find in your heart great peace.

REFLECTION: *Do I still believe "peace" will come only when I avenge myself on my enemies? Let me instead believe inner peace will come when I love my neighbor as myself.*

Hymn from the Akathist to the Theotokos

O victorious leader of triumphant hosts . . . as you possess invincible might, set us free from every calamity, so that we may sing: Rejoice, O Virgin and Unwedded Bride.

John of Kronstadt

John was born in 1829 in the Russian province of Archangelsk. He learned as a boy the power of intercessory prayer. After one long night of prayer, he found his persistent difficulty in learning to read had vanished; he could now read with clarity, as well as recall everything he studied in school. Eventually he was chosen to attend the Theological Academy in St. Petersburg—a high honor.

After marriage and ordination to the priesthood, he was sent to St. Andrew's Cathedral in the city of Kronstadt, a filthy, poverty- and disease-ridden naval base near St. Petersburg. He served his entire fifty-three-year ministry there.

Father John normally celebrated the Divine Liturgy daily, visited his flock, made sick calls, and spent time with people in the worst parts of town. He always received visitors and answered hundreds of appeals for spiritual and material help. He became known as a powerful intercessor and healer. He established workshops, a dormitory, and a school for the beggars of Kronstadt. He also gave remarkable advice that led to religious revival. He encouraged frequent Holy Confession and Holy Communion. During Great Lent, he often heard confessions from 2 PM to 2 AM. He would advise some penitents to better their lives even before they came to the sacraments.

During his last years, Fr. John predicted terrible events would befall Russia. His prophecy proved true during the period of communist rule. He died in 1909 and was glorified by the Russian Orthodox Church in 1990.

PRAYER: *Grant me strength, Lord, to persevere patiently and faithfully, wherever You may place me.*

SUNDAY   Fifth Week of Great Lent
Sunday of Saint Mary of Egypt
SCRIPTURE READING: MARK 10:32–45

Meditation

In today's reading, Jesus makes His final journey to Jerusalem before His Passion. He takes His twelve apostles aside and begins to tell them He will face betrayal, condemnation, and death—but He will rise again from the dead on the third day.

I wonder what my reaction would have been to my Master's words: fear? emptiness? anger? envy? Or would I have made the same request as did the Apostles James and John? They asked Jesus that they might "sit, one on Your right hand and the other on Your left, in Your glory" (Mark 10:37).

Immediately, Jesus tells them they do not realize what they are asking. The way to God's Kingdom is not what they would expect. The Kingdom is not a visible place on earth; nor does it provide an immediate, glorious worldly reward. One enters through many difficulties: suffering, struggles, persecutions, and tribulations. Jesus once told them the way to the Kingdom is narrow and difficult (see Matt. 7:13–14). The disciples did not understand this, and I admit I too would prefer a different answer!

Because the way of the world and the way of the Kingdom are in opposition, conflict swirls both inside and outside of me. Let me be willing to become a true servant of Christ. Let me be willing to drink of the Lord's cup (see Mark 10:38). In being faithful to the ways of heaven, let me enjoy its true power and unending bliss.

Font of Wisdom

Saint Innocent of Alaska (1797–1879), in his work *Indication of the Way to the Kingdom of Heaven*, strikingly compares "evil deeds" to "evil guards" that prevent the Holy Spirit from entering into the human heart. Among the worst of these he counts "bodily impurity and spiritual pride," which he claims are "especially repellent." Truly inviting the Holy Spirit into one's heart, he says, demands the following:

> *The true and recognized means of receiving the Holy Spirit, according to the teaching of the Holy Scripture and the experiences of great saints, are the following: purity of heart and chastity; humility; listening to the voice of God; prayer; daily self-denial; reading and listening to Holy Scripture; the sacraments of the Church and especially Holy Communion.*

REFLECTION: *According to society's mores, I count myself a decent person, but am I willing to become a person filled with the Spirit of God—a venture far more demanding?*

Hymn from Divine Liturgy

Having been a sinful woman, you became through repentance a bride of Christ. Having attained angelic life, you defeated demons with the weapon of the Cross. Therefore, O most glorious Mary, you are a bride of the Kingdom.

Venerable Mary of Egypt
COMMEMORATED APRIL 1/14
& FIFTH SUNDAY OF GREAT LENT

Mary lived from the mid-fourth to the early fifth century. She worked as a prostitute in the city of Alexandria for seventeen years—more to gratify her insatiable lust than to earn money. Out of curiosity, she once joined some pilgrims who were going to Jerusalem to celebrate the Feast of the Elevation of the Holy Cross. The ship's journey from Egypt did not interrupt her sinful lifestyle; she paid her passage by plying her trade.

Having disembarked in Jerusalem, she tried to enter the church with the rest of the throng for the festal celebration, but an invisible force held her back. Finally realizing her sinfulness, she prayed for help to the Virgin Mary and vowed to live a life of penance. In her prayer to the Mother of God, she was told to cross the Jordan River and to enter the desert.

Mary received Holy Communion at a church on the banks of the Jordan and then crossed the river into the wilderness, where for nearly forty-seven years she saw no other human being. She was tormented by physical needs and mental assaults, but she endured through the intercession of the Virgin Mary.

Around the year 430, the priest Zosimas—a hieromonk from a nearby monastery, who was on his annual Lenten retreat in the solitude of the desert—found Mary. She told him her story and asked him to tell no one about her until after her death. Zosimas promised to meet her a year later to give her Holy Communion. When he saw her the next Lent, she walked across the water of the Jordan to receive the Holy Eucharist. Then she walked back into the desert.

When Father Zosimas came back the following year, he discovered Mary had died, and he buried her body. Upon her repose, he was free to tell the world of her life.

PRAYER: *When I recognize the need but find it too difficult to change my life through repentance, help me to remember the courage of St. Mary of Egypt.*

MONDAY   Palm Week

SCRIPTURE READING: GENESIS 27:1–41

Meditation

The story of Isaac blessing his son Jacob illustrates the intense meaning of what we might think of as "mere words." I've often wondered: If Jacob deceived his father in order to receive his blessing, why couldn't Isaac take back the blessing and bestow it on his older son Esau? Why couldn't Isaac simply rescind his words?

The answer to my question lies in the fact that God's will is *always* accomplished—despite my human expectations, despite my sense of fairness. God knew the inner character of the two brothers. In His infinite wisdom, He chose Jacob to be the next patriarch. God knew Jacob's heart and found him worthy of this calling instead of Esau, who had rightful ownership of the blessing as the firstborn.

Two lessons are important for me here. The first is, God's will is always trustworthy, even when it does not coincide with my own will. The second is, my words and prayers, and my oaths and promises, will not be fulfilled unless they are congruent with God's will, no matter how beautiful, powerful, or truthful they may sound.

I confess that my wordy prayers—repeated with little care or diligence—often reflect my own will rather than God's will. They often mirror my complex wishes and hypocrisy rather than His simplicity and truth. My "mere words" will never find their fulfillment in God unless I become willing to listen to Him and to heed His word.

Font of Wisdom

In his *Homily III On the Statues,* St. John Chrysostom (347–407), the fiery archbishop of Constantinople, incisively defines true fasting:

> *Let the hands fast, by being pure from rapine and avarice.*
> *Let the feet fast, by ceasing from running to the unlawful spectacles.*
> *Let the eyes fast, being taught never to fix themselves rudely upon handsome countenances, or to busy themselves with strange beauties.*
> *Let the ear fast . . . refusing to receive evil speakings and calumnies.*
> *Let the mouth fast from disgraceful speeches and railings.*
> *For what doth it profit if we abstain from birds and fishes, and yet bite and devour our brethren?*

Saint John even demands proof from his listeners of true fasting! If you see a poor human being, take pity, he admonishes; and, he warns, beware of becoming envious if a friend is honored instead of yourself.

REFLECTION: *Have I reduced the definition of fasting to dietary rules during my Lenten sojourn? Or are my eyes, ears, feet, hands, and whole body fasting?*

Hymn from Vespers

Free us from soul-destroying greed, O Savior, and number us in the bosom of Abraham together with poor Lazarus, O You who for our sake became poor. You are rich in mercies. You lead us from corruption to incorruption, for You are a compassionate God, the lover of all.

New Hieromartyr Gregory V, Patriarch of Constantinople

Gregory was born in 1746 in the Peloponnesus region of Greece, a place his parents preferred to live in order to avoid oppression by the Ottoman Turks. Gregory was educated in Athens, Smyrna, and Patmos before becoming a monk.

Gregory gained an excellent reputation and became first chancellor, then metropolitan, of the archdiocese of Smyrna. Four years later, in 1797, he was elected to the patriarchal throne in Constantinople. During the troubled year that followed, he attempted to resist Turkish oppression while simultaneously endorsing patriotic factions on the Greek mainland. After trying to manage this volatile situation, he was deposed and deported to Mount Athos in 1798.

Recalled as patriarch in 1806, Gregory maintained a tenuous political balance between the Turks and Christians but was again expelled. He returned to Mount Athos in 1810. He was called for a third time to the patriarchal see in 1818, and in that year he became a member of the *Philiki Eteria* (Friendly Society), which was preparing for revolt against Turkish rule.

Greek revolts in the Peloponnesus eventually provoked reprisals. On March 25, 1821, Bishop Germanos of Patras led the Greeks in declaring independence from the Ottoman Turks. This declaration of Greek independence enraged the Turks, and they retaliated by seizing Gregory from his chambers and hanging him at the entrance of the patriarchate on the morning of April 10, Holy Pascha.

His body eventually was interred in the Church of the Annunciation, the Metropolitan Cathedral, in Athens. To this day, the center gate of the three main gates of the patriarchate, where Gregory was hanged, remains closed.

PRAYER: *Let me be a peacemaker, O Lord.*

TUESDAY Palm Week

SCRIPTURE READING: PROVERBS 21:3–21

Meditation

Chapter 21 of the Book of Proverbs considers society's relation-ship to the poor. Verse 13 warns, "Whoever shuts his ears to the cry of the poor / Will also cry himself and not be heard."

This passage pricks my conscience. As a steward of the gifts given to me by God, I am called to share them with the poor, cheerfully and without reluctance. Moreover, I am called to give even before satisfying all my own needs.

In the Gospel, Jesus speaks words parallel to those in Proverbs. He says, "inasmuch as you did *it* to one of the least of these My brethren, you did *it* to Me" (Matt. 25:40). Similarly, the Evangelist John writes, "But whoever has this world's goods, and sees his brother in need, and shuts up his heart from him, how does the love of God abide in him?" (1 John 3:17). Likewise, St. John Chrysostom teaches that no one can be saved without giving alms and without caring for the poor.

I often question whether or not the "needy" are merely lazy and just refuse to work. Still, I am called to love as God loves, and I can profess no real love if I do not share what I have with the poor. Along with my fasting and prayer during Great Lent, my giving to the poor must be done in secret. These are things I *can* do. These are things Jesus commands. What I must *not* do is close my ears to the cry of the poor.

Font of Wisdom

In a series of sermons about the "Parable of the Rich Man and Lazarus" (Luke 16:19–31), St. John Chrysostom (347–407) gives listeners insightful definitions of both wealth and poverty:

> *Let us learn not to call the rich lucky nor the poor unfortunate. Rather, if we are to tell the truth, the rich man is not the one who has collected many possessions but the one who needs few possessions; and the poor man is not the one who has no possessions but the one who has many desires.*

The saint astutely defines a greedy person as "the poorest of all"—one who is constantly "thirsting" for more. Similarly, he defines the person with few needs as "the richest of all"—one who is satisfied despite modest means.

REFLECTION: *I appreciate God's many blessings upon my life, but I still seek more—and even more! Let me assuage my nagging inner hunger by being satisfied with His presence, His love, alone.*

Hymn from Vespers

Today Lazarus has died; Bethany laments for him. But, Savior, You shall raise him from the dead, giving in Your friend assurance of Your awesome Resurrection, of the death of hell, and the life of Adam! Therefore we sing Your praises!

Sava I, Enlightener, First Archbishop of Serbia

Sava was born in 1175, the youngest son of Stephan I, who established a stable and continuous state for the Serbian people. At age 17, Sava became a monk on Mount Athos. After his father joined him, they together were granted the Hilandar Monastery on Mount Athos, which became a haven for monks of Serbian descent. Sava was ordained deacon and priest at this monastery. His monastic legacy includes the introduction of the Jerusalem *Typikon* (rubrics book) as the basis for Slavic monastic rules.

Sava returned home in 1208 to become superior of the Monastery of Studenica, a religious-political center of the emerging Serbian Church. He found Serbia in political and religious turmoil. The ecclesiastical and civil powers of Rome, Nicea, and Ochrid all seemed to threaten the young Serbian state. The Serbs needed their own bishops to educate the people, so Stephan II, Sava's brother, used his influence to make Sava the first archbishop of Serbia in 1219. Sava returned from his consecration in Nicea by way of Mount Athos, bringing home more monks and books from Hilandar. He then began to organize the Church and to help consolidate the state founded by his father.

After Sava died in Bulgaria in 1236, his body was taken to Milochevo Monastery in Serbia, where his veneration by people of all nationalities grew. During the Austrian-Turkish War in 1594, the Turks burned his relics. This allowed the Serbs to honor their beloved saint as a martyr as well.

PRAYER: *Lord, lead me on the path to Your Kingdom throughout my whole life.*

WEDNESDAY   Palm Week

SCRIPTURE READING: ISAIAH 58:1–12

Meditation

Today's passage from the Book of Isaiah warns about types of fasting displeasing and pleasing to God. Briefly, fasting that pleases God involves showing mercy to our brothers and sisters rather than parading our asceticism in public.

Likewise, Jesus warns, "Moreover, when you fast, do not be like the hypocrites, with a sad countenance. . . . But you, when you fast, anoint your head and wash your face, so that you do not appear to men to be fasting, but to your Father who *is* in the secret *place*; and your Father who sees in secret will reward you openly" (Matt. 6:16–18).

Both the Old and New Testaments instruct me in how to fast, emphasizing it as an important spiritual exercise. Similarly, from Holy Tradition I learn that fasting is not an end in itself, or a feat in which to take pride—after all, the demons are bodiless and never eat! Rather, fasting is a spiritual tool.

When I fast, I come to terms with my frailty, my mortality. I realize that without any food, I will die. I realize that with too much food I will sicken my body. I realize I have weak psychological and emotional resolve and an even weaker earthly body. In other words, I realize my total dependence on God for life. Fasting draws my attention away from earthly trappings that *"are* temporary," and helps me focus on the eternal "things which are not seen" as St. Paul says (see 2 Cor. 4:18). Through fasting, let me open my horizon; let me look heavenward.

127

Font of Wisdom

In his magnificent commentary titled "The Life of Moses," St. Gregory of Nyssa (c. 335–95) analyzes the passage in which God tells Moses, "you shall see My back; but my face shall not be seen" (Ex. 33:23)—lest the divine presence overwhelm the emboldened prophet and cause his death! Saint Gregory explains that following God requires looking only at the "back" of Him and keeping pace with Him "wherever He might lead."

> Someone who does not know the way cannot complete his journey safely in any other way than by following behind his guide. . . . He who follows will not turn aside from the right way if he always keeps the back of his leader in view. For he who moves to one side or brings himself to face his guide assumes another direction for himself than the one his guide shows him. Therefore, he says to the one who is led, My face is not to be seen, that is "Do not face your guide." If he does so, his course will certainly be in the opposite direction, for good does not look good in the face, but follows it.

The only safe road for a follower of Jesus, says St. Gregory, is to tread in the footsteps of the experienced Divine Guide.

REFLECTION: *I want either to run ahead of God, to demand of Him where He is headed, or to turn away from Him to go my own way. Will I trust my Divine Guide, as His footsteps lead me toward an unknown future via the way of the Cross?*

Hymn from Presanctified Liturgy

Now Lazarus has been in the tomb two days, beholding strange sights of terror. But Christ is coming to bring His friend to life, to implement in this one man His plan for all.

Moses the Ethiopian of Scete

Moses had been a servant in the house of an Egyptian official. After he was dismissed because of his continual thievery, he terrorized the area with a gang of robbers he had assembled. He was a strong, fierce, husky man and prone to an explosive temperament.

He was converted to Christianity in the late fourth century, possibly due to the influence of monastic hermits living in the desert, where Moses was hiding from the law. He became a monk at the monastery of Petra in western Egypt. On one occasion, four robbers attacked him in his cell. He overpowered them, tied them together in a sack, slung them across his back, and brought them to the elders of the monastery to hear their verdict on what to do with the brigands. The elders and Moses dealt so kindly with the thieves, they too repented and became monks.

Moses sometimes despaired of his past violent tendencies and former immorality. Eventually he calmed his passions by hard labor, waiting on his brothers, physical deprivation, and long prayer. After demonstrating much acquired humility, he was ordained as a deacon and then as a priest.

Prior to his death, Moses is said to have quoted Jesus' words, "for all who take the sword will perish by the sword" (Matt. 26:52), and he predicted their fulfillment in himself. Around the year 400, at about age seventy-five, Moses foresaw a raid on the monastery, and he urged his brother monks to flee rather than face certain death. Moses himself remained behind and was murdered. He was buried at the Monastery Dair al-Baramus in Egypt.

PRAYER: *Help me, O Lord, to transform my passionate nature through tears, humility, and diligent labor—just as St. Moses did.*

Meditation

Today's verses from Proverbs—"Do not be envious of evil men, / Nor desire to be with them; / For their heart devises violence, / And their lips talk of troublemaking" (24:1–2)—grab my attention. They also fill me with mixed emotions.

Often I envy those who seemingly live the good life—at least by worldly standards—despite their being unbelievers, nonchalant in the Faith, or even downright evil. I attend church services, but I resent those who don't. I fast from certain foods and forms of entertainment during Lenten seasons, but I am jealous of those who seem quite happy not to do so. "Why does Christianity, and especially Orthodoxy, have to be so *difficult?*" I grumble. I know Christ wants me to be pure of heart, mind, and soul, but it's more fun to eat, drink, and be merry! I envy those who are perfectly content, either unaware of or not desiring any spiritual struggle.

Then I remember: There is a difference between *happiness* and *joy*. "Rejoice and be exceedingly glad, for great *is* your reward in heaven," says Jesus in Matthew 5:12.

Material things may be desirable, even honorable, but they cannot replace the joy of the Spirit of God dwelling in my heart. Things that make me happy will fade away, but joy in my heart is irreplaceable—and eternal. Let me seek joy.

Font of Wisdom

The "prosperity gospel"—the belief that God wills only finan-
cial and physical well-being for His children—finds its roots in
nineteenth-century Protestant thought, but its shoots extend well
into the twenty-first century. In his writing *Indication of the Way into
the Kingdom of Heaven*, St. Innocent of Alaska (1797–1879) clarifies
the Orthodox Christian viewpoint on such matters:

> *To desire what is good for oneself and to seek prosperity or happi-
> ness is part of man's nature, and therefore it is not a sin or vice. But
> we need to know that here on earth there has not been, and is not,
> and never will be, true and perfect happiness and prosperity; for all
> our prosperity and happiness are only in God.*

The saint stresses that only God can quench the desires of the
human heart. "Do you want prosperity and happiness?" he asks.
"Seek it in God."

REFLECTION: *As I watch my Lord set His eyes toward Golgotha, let me
understand that true joy will come into my heart only by following His
footsteps to the Cross (see Luke 9:23).*

Hymn from Matins

*Let us come before the end of the fast with pure hearts . . . to the compas-
sionate God. Forgetting all cares of life, by abstinence, let us renounce our
love of pleasure and concern ourselves instead with charity.*

Martin the Confessor, Pope of Rome

Martin was a native of Umbria, in central Italy. His contemporaries regarded him as a priest of great intelligence, charity, and holiness. In 649 he was chosen to succeed Pope Theodore I as bishop of Rome.

During Martin's tenure as pope, the false doctrine of Monothelitism—which taught that Jesus Christ had only one will, instead of both a natural human will and a natural divine will—began to foment controversy. Both Emperor Constans II and Patriarch Paul of Constantinople embraced the doctrine, and they forbade disputes about it.

Knowing Monothelitism to be contrary to church dogma, however, Pope Martin lost no time in convening the Lateran Council and condemning the false doctrine as a heresy in 649. The enraged ruler had Martin seized, and the pope suffered many of the same torments His Savior had undergone: abuse, humiliation, and an unfair trial before his lying accusers. The only mercy Martin received was the kindness of his fellow prisoners while jailed, and the commutation of his death sentence to exile in Cherson in the Crimea. He died there in 655. The Sixth Ecumenical Council in 680–81 finally condemned the Monothelite teaching.

PRAYER: *When I feel discouraged or abandoned, Lord, let me remember You are always near, and You have shared in my suffering.*

Scripture Reading: Genesis 49:33—50:26

Meditation

The Book of Genesis ends with the death of the Jewish Patriarch Jacob, as well as his son Joseph. When Jacob dies, his sons, including Joseph, weep over him. Then, following Jacob's wishes, they carry his body to the land of Canaan for burial. The story concludes when Joseph dies and is buried in Egypt.

Strange, isn't it, that the Church prescribes a reading about two deaths on the last day of Great Lent? It would seem more appropriate to select a reading proclaiming the joy of accomplishing the forty-day fast.

But the wisdom of the Church is evident. Tomorrow is Lazarus Saturday, when Christ will weep over the death of His friend, then raise him from the tomb. Soon Jesus Himself will enter Jerusalem to be crucified and put to death prior to His own Resurrection.

Today's reading makes me ponder the connection between the deaths of Jacob and Joseph and the resurrections of Lazarus and Christ. Jacob's and Joseph's deaths remind me that death will someday touch me. Christ's Resurrection reminds me He has transformed death into an entryway into the Kingdom of His Father. His Resurrection has swallowed up death, making it impotent.

Great Lent has taught me to be faithful to Him. It has led me on a pilgrimage toward His everlasting Kingdom—which I experience even now, here on earth. Praise Him!

Font of Wisdom

In his First Epistle to the Corinthians, St. Paul admonishes his fellow Christians, "Therefore, whether you eat or drink, or whatever you do, do all to the glory of God" (10:31). Saint Basil the Great (329–79), hierarch and Cappadocian Father, takes up this theme in Question 5 of his *Greater Rules*, also known as the "Long Rules." He notes it is impossible to do Christian work properly unless it is carried out in accordance with the will of the One who orders it:

> *The smith in forging an axe, for example, thinks of the person who has commissioned the task, and with him in mind calculates its shape and size, suiting his work to the wish of him who ordered it done. (For if he is unmindful of this, he will fashion something different from what he was ordered to make.)*

By carrying out our work in accordance with God's will, says St. Basil, "we shall be linked to God in memory." In other words, whatever our task, we must keep God, our Master, in mind.

REFLECTION: *Jesus "steadfastly set His face" (Luke 9:51) toward the Holy City of Jerusalem to fulfill the will of His Father: death on the Cross. Let me also follow my Father's will, performing my everyday tasks for His glory.*

Hymn from Vespers

We have completed the forty days that profit our souls. Let us sing: Rejoice, Mary and Martha . . . tomorrow Christ will come and raise your dead brother to life. . . . Blessed is He that comes in the name of the Lord, the King of Israel.

Martyr Justin the Philosopher

COMMEMORATED JUNE 1/14

Justin, who lived in the second century, was a great Christian apologist, a defender of the Faith. Well educated in pagan philosophy, Justin was first drawn toward belief in Jesus Christ when he witnessed Christians facing martyrdom. Later, through further interactions with Christians, he studied Holy Scripture and learned more about the Faith. He was about thirty years old when he was baptized.

From that time on he journeyed throughout the Roman Empire, preaching the gospel. He also opened a school of Christian philosophy in Rome where religious beliefs were debated. Justin believed many others would gladly accept Christianity if it were properly explained to them. He considered it a Christian's duty to make the Faith known.

Remarkably, through one of his works defending Christianity, known as the *First Apology*, Justin persuaded the emperor to cease persecutions against Christians. In another work titled *Dialogue with Trypho the Jew* he illustrated the truth of Christianity on the basis of the writing of the prophets in the Old Testament. Justin addressed his *Second Apology* to the Roman Senate.

Justin was arrested after a public argument with a Roman cynic, Crescentius. After making a bold confession and refusing to sacrifice to the gods, he was beheaded in 165.

PRAYER: *Lord, help me to proclaim clearly and accurately my faith in You, relying on You to help me find the appropriate words.*

Feast of the Annunciation of the Theotokos
March 25/April 7
Scripture Reading: Hebrews 2:11–18

Meditation

God's Incarnation—the Word of God becoming human—astounds me. Yet today's epistle declares He became like human beings in every respect, so He might be a "merciful and faithful High Priest in things *pertaining* to God" (Heb. 2:17).

I am struck with wonder when I see the glory of God's creation: gorgeous sunrises, thousands of brilliant stars on a cold winter night, intricate geometric patterns in nature. I am equally awed when I consider that God, who created such wonders, became incarnate to renew and reunite all of creation—including me—with Himself.

Even more amazing, I worship a God who has felt not only love, joy, and peace, but also anger, rejection, and loneliness, as well as every human temptation (Heb. 4:15). Jesus of Nazareth experienced my every emotion. Because He experienced suffering and temptation without sinning, Jesus can help me overcome my sins. Because He died for me, He has set me free from the "fear of death" that kept me in bondage (Heb. 2:15). This incomprehensible mystery overwhelms me.

The Incarnation was made possible by the response of the Virgin Mary to the archangel: "Let it be to me according to your word" (Luke 1:38). Cooperating with God's plan, she gave God's Divine Son our human nature. On this day I am thankful to the Almighty Trinity and to the Virgin Mary for inaugurating my salvation.

Font of Wisdom

Jesus Christ told His followers, "Blessed *are* the pure in heart, / For they shall see God" (Matt. 5:8). Saint Gregory (c. 335–95), bishop of Nyssa, in his work *On Virginity*, writes about the difficulty of conveying the meaning of this beatitude to anyone consumed by dark motives. The saint compares God's glory to sunshine:

> *If a man has not seen it [sunshine] since his earliest days, any effort to translate the experience into words is useless and meaningless. You cannot make the brilliance of the sunlight shine through his ears. And so it is with the true light of the Spirit. Each man needs his own eyes to see its beauty.*

Saint Gregory claims people who lack integrity and purity of heart have a "glaze over the window of the soul." Only by intentionally struggling to remove that stubborn veneer will they become capable of beholding God.

REFLECTION: *As I commemorate the Mother of God—honored for her integrity and purity of soul and body—let me beg her intercession in removing "glazes" of dishonesty, double-mindedness, and ill intent that obscure my soul and prevent me from beholding God.*

Festal Hymn

Today is the beginning of our salvation, the revelation of the eternal mystery. The Son of God becomes the Son of the Virgin as Gabriel announces the coming of grace. Together with Him let us cry to the Theotokos: Rejoice, O full of grace, the Lord is with you.

Feast of the Annunciation of the Theotokos
(Virgin Mary, Mother of God)

The name "Mary" (a variation of the Hebrew *Mariam*) has many meanings: "wished-for child," "beloved," and "bitter," among them. All of these apply to the Blessed Virgin Mary, who gave birth to the Christ Child. Mary's parents, Joachim and Anna, were barren until their older years, and they longed and wished for a child; Mary was beloved and highly favored by God; and Mary endured bitter suffering in her heart upon seeing her only Son crucified on the Cross.

Some of Mary's life is recorded in Scripture. However, Church Tradition offers further details, found both in the teachings of the Church Fathers and in the apocryphal writing *The Protoevangelium of St. James.*

Today's reading from the Gospel of Luke (1:24–49, 56) offers a rich and full description of the Annunciation itself. Gabriel assures Mary that her newborn Son will be "the Son of the Highest" (v. 32) and that "of His kingdom there will be no end" (v. 33). In response to the archangel's greeting, Mary says, "Behold the maidservant of the Lord! Let it be to me according to your word" (v. 38). Additionally, the archangel Gabriel's words to Mary fulfill the prophecy of Isaiah: "Therefore the Lord Himself will give you a sign: Behold, the virgin shall conceive and bear a Son, and shall call His name Immanuel" (Is. 7:14).

This feast celebrates the divine–human cooperation that brings salvation to the human race. The Son of God becomes the Son of Mary, taking our human form and sharing in our flesh and blood (see Heb. 2:14). In return, He grants Mary, and all of humanity, the possibility of sharing in His divine life—as long as each person answers His call with a resounding "Let it be."

PRAYER: *Most Holy Mother of God, pray that I too may open my heart and answer "Yes" when the Lord calls on me to do His will.*

Epilogue

Memory Eternal, Archpriest Steven John Belonick*

A few weeks before he died of acute myeloid leukemia, my husband Steven spoke of trust in God. Over the past year we had talked of many things—from the latest chemotherapy treatments available to possibly relocating to a more accessible home in a milder climate—hopeful topics. But now, the time had come. Now, we spoke of death.

I asked him if he feared death, feared facing judgment by our Lord Jesus Christ. He replied, "I know that all the sins I have committed, the saints tell me, are like a drop of water compared to God's compassion. He can look past all that, and He can see what's really in my heart. I trust Him. I simply trust *in* Him. He's never been untrustworthy before; why would He be so now?"

He didn't say this lightly (even admitting his childlike and perhaps naïve attitude), but he did say it with a firm hope, even with a sense of anticipation. He then spoke of a specific time in which God had shown him His trustworthiness, a time that had sealed Steven's certitude in Him:

---

* Quotations are taken from conversations recorded by Fr. Steven's wife, Deborah, during his last days, with the intention of sharing them with her sons and their families; he was unaware she was recording.

At one point in my ministry, I was feeling that I was a failure. And I got this emergency telephone call to visit someone; he was in Wilson Hospital dying. The family was there when I arrived, and I stayed with them until the person passed. It was three o'clock in the morning when I arrived, and when I left, the sun was just coming up. There was nothing more for them that I could do. As I left the hospital, I was overcome by this sense of Presence, and you can say, "Wow, that's just your imagination, or whatever," but it was more than that. And this Presence spoke to me, and what this Presence said was, "This is where I called you; this is where I called you to serve Me; be quiet, shut up, Steven."

And whenever I would have that feeling sometimes of loss after that, then I would always remember that moment, and it was a reminder to me: This is who I am; God called me to be His servant in this very particular special way. And every time I read the Scripture of that event [between the risen Lord and the disciple Peter (John 21:15–17), in which Jesus asks Peter to follow Him and to feed His sheep], it is those words that have so much meaning to me, because it feels like it's a directive, like I was in Peter's shoes. And, like Peter, I have no fancy background, no special talent. I just wanted to serve Him because I love Him. It gives me such a sense of peace, such a sense of being loved. It was in response to His love.

Steven also spoke of the "cutting away" now required of him. He talked of all the risks he had undertaken when he had decided to enter the priesthood, all he had had to cut away and leave behind. He said those experiences led up to the final risk he now was facing: deciding to halt the chemotherapy that ravaged his body without any healing effect. This time he would be leaving behind his wife and his sons, daughters-in-law (whom he endearingly called "my girls"), and grandchildren to enter a new realm. Only one thing made this final, severe cut bearable, he said: "Because what I anticipate is being embraced by the One who has never hurt me, always did the best for me, and always loved me more than I deserve. That's what I wait for, so it's okay."

Each meditation in this little book reminds me of lessons taught me by Steven throughout my life with him, but especially during his last days. Each requires a cutting away of worldly cares, and each requires a building up of trust in God. Most importantly, each requires a *surrender* to the One who is all-embracing Love.

May we all continue our pilgrimage to Pascha, passing from death to life, until our last day.

Christ is risen. Risen Indeed!

—Deborah (Malacky) Belonick

Bibliography with Notes

References for the "Font of Wisdom" sections are cited here. The Week/Day corresponding to each source is also noted; where more than one source is possible, the Week/Day is noted twice. References also may apply to some quotations in the sections recounting the lives of the saints.

Basil the Great. *Ascetical Works,* The Fathers of the Church Series. vol. 9. Translated by Sister M. Monica Wagner, C.S.C. Washington, DC: The Catholic University of America Press, 1962.
* Basil the Great. *The Long Rules.* "Preface." pp. 224–25.—Week 1/ Tuesday
* Basil the Great. *The Long Rules.* Question 5: "On Avoiding Distraction." p. 244.—Palm Week/Friday

Bolshakoff, Serge. *Russian Mystics.* Kalamazoo, MI: Cistercian Publications, 1980.
* Theophan the Recluse. pp. 210–11.—Week 3/Thursday

Brianchaninov, Bishop Ignatius. *On the Prayer of Jesus.* Liberty, TN: Saint John of Kronstadt Press, 1995.
* Ignatius Brianchaninov. pp. 43–44.—Week 5/Thursday

Chariton of Valaamo, Igumen. *The Art of Prayer: An Orthodox Anthology.* Edited by F. Kadloubovsky and translated by E.M. Palmer. Edited with an introduction by Timothy Ware. Paperback edition. New York: Farrar, Straus and Giroux, 1997.
* Theophan the Recluse. p. 53.—Week 3/Saturday

Churchill, Leigh. *The Birth of Europe*. Milton Keynes, UK: Paternoster Press, 2001.
+ Alexis, the Man of God. p. 174.—Week 5/Wednesday (in life of the saint section)

de Catanzaro, C.J. *Symeon the New Theologian: The Discourses*, Classics of Western Spirituality Series. Ramsey, NJ: Paulist Press, 1980.
+ Symeon the New Theologian. *Discourse I, Of Charity* §3: "Charity is altogether desirable." p. 43.—Day before Great Lent
+ Symeon the New Theologian. *Discourse XXXVI, In the Form of a Thanksgiving [at the Threshold of Total Illumination]* §10: "For the Resplendence of the Vision of God." pp. 374–75.—Week 3/Monday
+ Symeon the New Theologian. *Discourse XVII, On Worthy and Unworthy Superiors* §14: "God Increases Virtue." pp. 219–20.
  —Week 4/Tuesday

Gregory of Nyssa. *From Glory to Glory: Texts from St. Gregory of Nyssa's Mystical Writings*. Introduction by Jean Daniélou. Translated by Herman Musurillo. Crestwood, NY: St. Vladimir's Seminary Press, 1995.
+ Gregory of Nyssa. *On Virginity*. pp. 112–17.—Week 1/Wednesday
+ Gregory of Nyssa. *On Virginity*. pp. 104–5.—Feast of the Annunciation

Gregory of Nyssa. *The Life of Moses*, Classics of Western Spirituality Series. Translated by Abraham Malherbe and Everett Ferguson. Ramsey, NJ: Paulist Press, 1978. Published in cooperation with Cistercian Publications Inc., Kalamazoo, MI, and is Number 31 in their series, Cistercian Studies.
+ Gregory of Nyssa. *The Life of Moses* §II:251–53. pp. 119–20.
  —Palm Week/Wednesday

Gregory Palamas. *The Triads*, Classics of Western Spirituality Series. Translated by Nicholas Gendle. Ramsey, NJ: Paulist Press, 1982.
+ Gregory of Palamas. *The Triads* §II.ii.20. pp. 47–48, 55.—Week 2/Sunday

Grisbrooke, W. Jardine. *Father John of Kronstadt: Spiritual Counsels.* Selected passages from *My Life in Christ.* Crestwood, NY: St. Vladimir's Seminary Press, 1966.
+ John of Kronstadt. p. 11.—Week 3/Tuesday
+ John of Kronstadt. pp. 164–66.—Week 3/Friday
+ John of Kronstadt. pp. 4–6.—Week 5/Wednesday
+ John of Kronstadt. pp. 184–85.—Week 5/Saturday

Innocent, Bishop of Kamchatka, the Kurilian and Aleutian Islands. *Indication of the Way into the Kingdom of Heaven.* Pamphlet. Jordanville, NY: Holy Trinity Monastery; Printshop of St. Job of Pochaev, 1994.
+ Innocent of Alaska. Part Four (6): "How Jesus Christ Helps Us to Go the Way into the Kingdom of Heaven, and How We Can Receive His Help." p. 32.—Week 4/Friday
+ Innocent of Alaska. Part Four (7). p. 34.—Week 5/Sunday
+ Innocent of Alaska. Introduction. pp. 1–2.—Palm Week/Thursday

Isaac the Syrian. *The Ascetical Homilies of St. Isaac the Syrian.* Translation by Holy Transfiguration Monastery. Boston: Holy Transfiguration Monastery, 1984.
+ Isaac the Syrian. *Homily III:* "On the Senses and on Temptations Also." p. 24.—Week 2/Saturday
+ Isaac the Syrian. *Homily XLVI:* "Containing Profitable Subjects Replete with the Wisdom of the Spirit." p. 224.—Week 1/Saturday & Week 5/Monday

John Chrysostom. *On Wealth and Poverty,* Popular Patristics Series. vol. 9. Translated by Catherine P. Roth. Crestwood, NY: St. Vladimir's Seminary Press, 1999.
+ John Chrysostom. "The Parable of the Rich Man and Lazarus." p. 40.—Palm Week/Tuesday

John Chrysostom. *St. John Chrysostom, Homilies on Genesis 1–17,* The Fathers of the Church Series. vol. 74. Translated by Robert C. Hill. Washington, DC: The Catholic University of America Press, 1986.
+ John Chrysostom. *Homily XVII.11, 12.* p. 227.—Week 1/Friday

John Climacus. *The Ladder of Divine Ascent*, Classics of Western Spirituality Series. Translated by Colm Luibheid and Norman Russell. Introduction by Kallistos Ware. Mahwah, NJ: Paulist Press, 1982.
+ John Climacus. Step 26: "On Discernment." p. 251—Week 4/ Wednesday
+ John Climacus. Step 28: "On Prayer." pp. 275–76, and Introduction, p. 45.—Week 4/Sunday

Manual of Communion Prayers of the Orthodox Church, A, vol. 1. Compiled by the Community of the Holy Myrrhbearers. Introduction by Archpriest Thomas Hopko. Otego, NY: Community of the Holy Myrrhbearers, 1994.
+ Symeon the New Theologian. p. 28.—Week 1/Sunday (in life of the saint section)

Maximus the Confessor. *Maximus Confessor: Selected Writings*, Classics of Western Spirituality Series. Edited by George Charles Berthold. Mahwah, NJ: Paulist Press, rev. ed., 1985.
+ Maximus the Confessor. *Third Century*: §§47, 48. p. 67.—Week 2/ Monday

Philokalia, The: The Complete Text, vol. IV. Compiled by St. Nikodimos of the Holy Mountain and St. Makarios of Corinth. Translated from the Greek by G.E.H. Palmer, Philip Sherrard, and Kallistos Ware. London: Faber and Faber Ltd., 1995.
+ Gregory of Sinai. *On the Signs of Grace and Delusion, Written for the Confessor Longinos: Ten Texts*. Text 9: "On Divine Energy." p. 262.—Week 4/Thursday

Select Library of Nicene and Post-Nicene Fathers of the Christian Church, A, First Series (NPNF[1]). Edited by Philip Schaff. 1886–89. 14 vols. Repr. Peabody, MA: Hendrickson, 1994.
+ John Chrysostom. Vol. 9. *Homily On the Statues III.7.*—Week 1/ Monday
+ John Chrysostom. Vol. 13. *Homily On 1 Timothy 3:8–10 XI.Moral.* —Week 5/Friday
+ John Chrysostom. Vol. 9. *Homily On the Statues III.11.*—Palm Week/Monday

Select Library of Nicene and Post-Nicene Fathers, A, Second Series
(NPNF²). Edited by Philip Schaff and Henry Wace. Translated by
Charles G. Browne and James E. Swallow. Buffalo, NY: Christian
Literature Publishing Co., 1894.
+ Gregory Nazianzen. Vol. 7. *Oration 43.*—Week 2/Tuesday (in life
of the saint section)

Seraphim of Sarov. *The Little Russian Philokalia, Volume I: St. Seraphim
of Sarov.* Translated by Seraphim Rose. Platina, CA: St. Herman of
Alaska Press, 1994.
+ Seraphim of Sarov. *Guarding the Heart* §26. p. 46.—Week 1/
Thursday
+ Seraphim of Sarov. *Discernment of the Heart's Workings* §27. pp.
46–47. —Week 2/Wednesday
+ Seraphim of Sarov. *Prayer* §10. p. 29.—Week 4/Saturday

Sherwood, Polycarp. *St. Maximus the Confessor: The Ascetic Life; The Four
Centuries on Charity,* Ancient Christian Writers Series. Pine Beach,
NJ: Newman House, 1995.
+ Maximus the Confessor. *The Ascetic Life* §41. p. 132.—Week 2/
Tuesday

Theophan the Recluse. *Unseen Warfare: The Spiritual Combat and Path
to Paradise of Lorenzo Scupoli.* Edited by Nicodemus of the Holy
Mountain and revised by Theophan the Recluse. Translated by E.
Kadloubovsky and G. E. H. Palmer. Introduction by H.A. Hodges.
Crestwood, NY: St. Vladimir's Seminary Press, 1978.
+ Theophan the Recluse, Ed. Chapter 45: "Our Severe Judgment of
Others Comes from a High Opinion of Ourselves and the Instiga-
tion of the Devil. How to Overcome This Tendency." p. 197.—Week
2/Thursday
+ Theophan the Recluse, Ed. *Ibid.* p. 198.—Week 2/Friday

Theophan the Recluse. *The Path of Prayer: Four Sermons on Prayer.* First
Edition. Edited by Robin Amis. Translated by Esther Williams. Her-
mitage, TN: Praxis Institute Press, 1992.
+ Theophan the Recluse. *Third Sermon:* "Unceasing Prayer." p. 20.
—Week 1/Sunday

+ Theophan the Recluse. *First Sermon*: "A Personal Rule of Prayer."
pp. 2–3.—Week 3/Sunday
+ Theophan the Recluse. *First Sermon*: "A Personal Rule of Prayer."
pp. 3–4.—Week 4/Monday

Tikhon of Zadonsk. *Journey to Heaven: Counsels on the Particular Duties of
Every Christian*. Translated by Fr. George D. Lardas. Jordanville, NY:
Holy Trinity Monastery; Printshop of St. Job of Pochaev, 1991; third
printing 2004.
+ Tikhon of Zadonsk. *Part III: Spiritual Struggles*, Chapter 8: "Sins of
the Tongue" §38: "Do not slander and do not judge." pp. 78–79.
—Week 3/Wednesday

Ware, Kallistos. *How to Read Your Bible*, Ancient Faith Topical Series.
Chesterton, IN: Ancient Faith Publishing, 1988.
+ Tikhon of Zadonsk. p. 1—Week 5/Tuesday